Mental Hijrah

Towards a Unified Muslim World-View

It is understood that Quranic Ayahs deliver their message within a context. Besides, there is a "sea of concepts" that provides the "living" background for the individual Surahs of Quran and the individual Ayahs of the Surahs. This background is alive with overarching themes that provide the dynamism for the Surahs and Ayahs to interact coherently to produce "a symphony of nature" with which life of a person and life of a society resonate. This living background is referred to as the "Hikmah" of Quran, and it is an integral part of Quranic guidance. I have formulated some content of this "Hikmah" in the form of formally enunciated "Theorems". It is the first formulation, ever, for the Hikmah in Quran.

The book is divided into five parts, each called a book. We start with the book of Framework, which describes the problem this book attempts to resolve, an approach to the solution, the tools available to achieve the solution, and an architectural framework in which to implement the solution. It is commonly understood that the foundation of Islam is on its five pillars. The framework defines the architecture that the five pillars need to support. Without such architecture, the pillars just stand there aimlessly. Next comes the book of Worships, which examines the worships that Quran prescribes. These worships are performed in physical, ethical, and spiritual dimensions. The worships in the spiritual dimension include the well-known five pillars of Islam, and they also include worships in the physical and ethical dimensions, as well as worships at the level of the Ummah, which are currently neglected with impunity. Next comes the book of Wisdom, which consists of a set of "theorems" that attempt to enunciate aspects of the "Hikmah" in Quran. This is followed by the book of Research, which discusses and formulates a number of research problems in various categories. The Muslim researchers are invited to address this catalogue of research problems. Finally, we conclude with the book of Vision, which compares the Muslim world-view and the Euro-American world-view and suggests how each can benefit from the other.

The second edition has, to some extent, sharpened its focus on two facets. One is the decadent nature of sectarianism that some Ulama uphold, but Quran denounces. Second is the role of the Ummah among the nations of the world. The action plan derives from the Hikmah of Quran which is essential to understand Quran and properly make it actionable in a programmatic sense, given a specific space-time environment.

I aspire that this book will help the Muslims and the Ummah to embark on the path of the Quranic Hikmah, so that the sun will shine for them and bring forth their Renaissance. Please accept this second edition of Mental Hijrah: Towards a Unified Muslim World-View. We offer it to all readers, especially to the youth who have an upwelling thirst in their hearts and minds to find out the truth about Islam.

Mental Hijrah

Towards a Unified Muslim World-View

Abdur Rahim Choudhary

Muslim Voice

MV Publishers

Published by MV Publishers, a subsidiary of Muslim Voice,
12719 Hillmeade Station Dr, Bowie, MD 20720, USA.

MVPublishers@muslimvoice.org

First edition 2003
ISBN 81-86632-84-0

Second edition 2022
ISBN 978-1-956601-06-0

United States of America

Choudhary, Abdur Rahim, 1944–
Mental Hijrah, Towards a Unified Muslim World-View

2nd Edition
ISBN 978-1-956601-06-0

To
> my parents Ali Mohammad Choudhary
> and Khadija Begum Choudhary,
> my soulmate Yasmeen Sultana Choudhary,
> my children Rehan, Saba, Farhan and Adnan,
> and my grandchildren Ishmal and Humza; Sana and Sulaiman.

Content

Preface to the second edition

Allah be praised, nineteen years have passed since the first edition of this book was published. This second edition has become necessary because the book has been out of print. I have taken the opportunity to enhance the presentation of the book. The foremost change is to incorporate the footnotes within the main text of the book so that it is easy on the reader to go through a more continuous narrative, versus having to divert to the notes and then revert back to the main text. We have also taken the opportunity to reorganize the material. Book sections that introduced different books are now included into the chapters themselves. Other changes include a different font set, fewer headings, and a slightly larger page size.

This somewhat revised second edition has, to a slightly greater extent, sharpened its focus on two facets. One is the decadent nature of sectarianism that some Ulama uphold, but Quran denounces. Second is the role of the Ummah among the nations of the world. The action plan derives from the Hikmah of Quran which is emphasized as essential to understand Quran and properly make it actionable in a programmatic sense, given a specific space-time environment.

The sections on the role of the Angels, the discourse on Taqwa, and the theorems in the book of Hikmah have now evolved into an axiomatic theory of spirituality which will soon be published as a separate book. I have presented spirituality as a separate and independent discipline, not as an annex to a religion, as it is presently studied. I deem this new book to be an introduction to the path of Sufism without any specific Tariqa.

I aspire that this second edition will help the Muslims and the Ummah to embark on the path of the Quranic Hikmah, so that the sun will shine for them. Please accept this second edition of Mental Hijrah: Towards a Unified Muslim World-View. We offer it to everyone, especially to the youth who have an upwelling thirst in their hearts and minds to know the truth about Islam.

Abdur Rahim Choudhary
Muslim Voice
12719 Hillmeade Station Dr, Bowie, MD 20720, USA.
September 22, 2022.

Preface to the first edition

Please accept this effort from me for the Revival of the Muslim World-View. This objective is sought via a framework that I refer to as a Mental Hijrah: a migration in the intellectual plane. The framework is the result of the harmony that I strived to create in my life as a human being, a Muslim, and a scientist. The task was gigantic, but I took the first step. Thanks be to Allah; I made some headway during a long period of experiences and analysis. If I were to summarize the results in one word, it boils down to "Taqwa". The book indeed presents a detailed theory of Taqwa, which is a step towards understanding the formal theory of spirituality as embodied in Quranic Hikmah and the Prophetic Sunnah.

However, that was the easier part. When it comes to creating harmony in a society, and the World at large, the task is indeed daunting. I share with you the results that my own research has produced so far. Again, if I were to summarize the results, the key concepts are those that Quran describes as "Ummah", "Khilafah" and "Shura". I have developed a theory based on these concepts, and I share it with you as you accompany me through the pages of this book.

In the course of my research, I found the guidance of Quran invaluable. I consulted the Hadith material as well. To my surprise, I found that Quran sufficed for my research thus far. Therefore, you will find that all my references on the Islamic concepts are to the Ayahs of Quran. The translation of Quran that I have used is from "The Meaning of THE HOLY QUR'AN" by Abdullah Yusuf Ali, Amana Publication, ISBN 0-915957-76-0. Occasionally I have used the translation by Mohammad Asad, and those occasions are explicitly so identified.

There is a challenge here. We all know that Quranic Ayahs deliver their message-content within a context. Besides the context, there is a "sea of concepts" that provides the "living" background for the individual Surahs of Quran and the individual Ayahs of the Surahs. This background is alive with overarching themes. These provide the dynamism for the Surahs and Ayahs to interact coherently to produce "a symphony of nature" with which the life of a person as well as the life of a society resonates. This living background is referred to as the "Hikmah", and it is an integral part of Quranic guidance. I have attempted to express some contents of this "Hikmah" that are important in today's space-time. This is done in the form of some formally enunciated "Theorems".

The research work reported in this book, like any other research, is a work in progress. I invite you to develop it farther. For that reason, I have identified some topics of research that would help the Muslims and the Ummah in the space-time of today.

This work is divided into five parts, each called a book. We start with the book of Framework, which describes the problem this research attempts to resolve, an approach to the solution, the tools available to achieve the solution, and an architectural framework in which to implement the solution. It is commonly understood that the foundation of Islam is on its five pillars. The framework defines the architecture that the five pillars need to support. Next comes the book of Worships, which examines the worships that Quran prescribes.

These include the worships in the physical, ethical, and spiritual dimensions. The worships in the spiritual dimension include the well-known five pillars of Islam, and they also include the currently neglected worships at the level of the Ummah. Next comes the book of Wisdom, which consists of a set of "theorems" that attempt to enunciate aspects of the "Hikmah" in Quran, in the context of today's space-time. This is followed by the book of Research, which discusses and formulates a number of research problems in various categories. The Muslim researchers are invited to extend this work by addressing this catalogue of research problems. Finally, we conclude with the book of Vision, which compares the Muslim world-view and the Euro-American world-view and suggests how each can benefit from the other.

Abdur Rahim Choudhary
6426 Grendel Place, Bowie, Maryland 20720, USA.
May 15, 2002.

1 Quranic Framework

Allah's name is what I begin this effort with. In His glory and love I seek guidance.

In order to understand the message in Quran, and to seek guidance from it, we first need to know the 'Framework' that outlines an architectural scheme required to build a well guided person and a just society, in order to bring peace and prosperity to mankind. This Quranic framework is clearly stated in Quran 51:56: "I have only created Jinns and men that they may serve me".

The Quranic framework consists of service to Allah, also called the "worship of Allah". This framework helps us to understand and communicate the basic teachings of Quran within the big picture of its grand scheme of things.

The modules of Quranic framework consist of the worships of Allah in three dimensions, namely the physical, ethical, and spiritual dimensions. As we will discuss in chapter 2, worships in the three dimensions are abundantly described, and clearly illustrated, in Quran.

These three dimensions are "independent", which means that the three dimensions exist in an intrinsic way and cannot be reduced to a smaller number. The desired effects intended by Quran cannot be achieved if any one of the dimensions is neglected or inadequately represented. Therefore, they together define the framework envisioned in Quran.

The predicament of Muslims today arises from not being heedful of this essential requirement of the Quranic framework. For example, if we neglect the worship of Allah in the physical dimension, the intended peace and prosperity will illude us. Similarly, if we neglect the worships of Allah in ethics dimension within our society, then too the desired peace and prosperity will illude us. We must pay heed to the physical world, the ethical excellence, and the spiritual dimension in order to achieve peace and prosperity, and deserve to be the Khalifah.

Chapter 1 presents a detailed analysis of this failure of Muslims in understanding the Quranic framework. Chapter 2 presents a solution to the current predicament of Muslims using Quranic framework. The detailed solution presented in Chapter 2 uses an architecture based on the three modules of Quranic framework. Chapters 1 and 2 together constitute what we call the "Book of Framework".

1.1 Muslims of today

We ponder over the beauty of Islam. This is the beauty that arises from a world of Peace: the world that is within each one of us, and a world that is around each one of us. This allows us to comprehend Muslims, the followers of Islam. Islam is an ever-flowing fountain of strength for its followers, "strength" in every sense: physical, ethical, and spiritual. Muslims display this strength in circumstances that are favorable to them as well as in those that are extremely arduous. Islam gives the Muslims a generous and sharing heart in good times, and an amazing grace in the face of extreme odds.

Muslims today number over two billions among a world of about seven billions. If numbers were a criterion, Muslims would already be a most significant factor in shaping the world of today. It does not take a complicated analysis to realize that this is not the case. Muslims today matter in shaping the events of the world to a far lesser extent than what one might expect considering their numbers, distribution, and resources.

Is this a normal circumstance with Muslims? The answer is a resounding no!

The Prophet (S) made a significant effort to shape the world according to the ideology of Islam. He shaped all aspects of the world of his time, including spiritual, financial, political, defense, and human dimensions. The Caliphs (R) continued this strategy. They implemented it over an ever-increasing part of the world.

Even the ruling dynasties that followed the Caliphs (R) did not significantly reduce this scope of the Muslim life. Please note that dynasties is a collective reference to the Muslim rulers that followed the era of the four Caliphs. The Muslims have been the flag bearers of peace and prosperity for the world and the champions of human values for all the peoples.

Why then do the Muslims matter so little in the world of today?

For a clue to this important question let us look at the advent of the industrial revolution, after the advent of renaissance in Europe. It changed the world remarkably. This change was not just in terms of the machines that impacted the patterns of life, but also in terms of the outlook of the people of the world.

The change in the mental outlook was unfortunately in opposite directions, as it happened in the Euro-American people and as it occurred in the Muslim people.

The European people performed a change in their world-view. Instead of being the followers of dogmas, they started to harness the forces of nature. The European masses liberated themselves from the exploitation of the despotic rulers on one hand, and the excesses of the Clergy on the other.

They started to think for themselves.

This was in contra distinction to blindly following the dictates of the 'people of authority' in the name of the Sovereign, or following the demands of the Clergy in the name of God.

It was during the same era that the Muslim world-view significantly deviated from the vision of the Prophet, Mohammad (S) son of Abdullah. This vision is built on the concept of Tauheed, which in a simplistic way means that the single (indivisible) entity cannot be analyzed into constituents without introducing serious errors in the understanding of the nature of the entity. When the concept is applied to the human life, it means that the life must be treated as a whole without dividing it into isolated compartments, for example the government and the religion.

This concept started to weaken after the time of the Caliphs (R). The reasons are many. One reason is the fact that the reign under the dynasties was a significant departure from the political system envisioned by the Prophet (S) and exemplified by the Caliphs (R). This circumstance started to show strains on Muslim individuals and in

Muslim society. It came to a stage where Muslims subscribed to Tauheed in intellectual terms, while they experienced a de-facto separation between the political realities and the religious convictions. The minds were polarized under the pressures of the political authority on one hand, and on the other the pressures of having to choose between an ever-increasing number of mutually conflicting schools of religious thought. This mental polarization reached epidemic proportions during the colonial era that followed the industrial revolution. No relief was available to Muslims either on a personal level or at a national level. The Muslims felt politically helpless because the system provided them no reasonable means to impact the state of affairs. They also felt incapacitated in making the right choice between the religious doctrines. As a result, they stopped thinking for themselves and started to blindly submit to the political and religious authorities.

The Muslim mindset changed from a thinking and analyzing mind, which is what Quran requires, to a mindset of blind following. At the same time, the European mindset changed from a blind following to a mindset of enquiry and analysis.

The Muslims of today are quite different from those in the era of the Prophet (S).

The Prophet used Quran as a roadmap and a pragmatic guidance in all his affairs. Above all, the Prophet had a well-defined objective in everything he did. There never was a separation of his activities into worship and secular matters. Every activity was both. He freely allowed the focus of his activities to be modulated by the events on the ground.

Muslims of today contrast this situation, almost occupying a diametrically opposite position. They tend to divide life into worship and secular aspects. Thus, the modern learning consisting of science, technology, arts, and humanities is largely ascribed a secular significance. Practices such as the prayer, fasting, pilgrimage, and charity are regarded with religious significance. The mindset is occupied in defining these contradistinctions. The focus on pragmatic objectives is completely lost. The realities on the ground are not allowed to influence this outlook and mindset.

The outcome of this contrast is also very visible. The Prophet used Quranic guidance and took the Muslims to the peaks of glory, in spiritual sense as well as in secular sense. Muslims of today have made Quran into rigid shackles to keep their feet tied firmly. They do not know spirituality; their focus is a confused desire to escape the fear of hell. They also do not possess the secular glory, as they spend their energies in sectarian pursuits.

As the above discussion shows the problem with the Muslims today is their mindset. Their thinking is polarized, trying in vain to define contradistinctions between matters of spirituality and those belonging to this world. They adhere to the religious rituals out of a fear of punishment, rather than a love for the positive message of Quran. They have made the guidance of Quran into shackles on their feet, and the guidance of the Sunnah into a circus for the sectarians.

1.2 Correcting the mindset

It is true that the predicament of Muslims today is not a happy one. What is even truer is that it is now time for the Muslims to revert back to the glory that is, by design, their lot. This means, as discussed in the previous section, that the Muslims need to make a mental Hijrah. This migration is from a blind submission to the political and religious authorities, to a Quranic mindset that inquires and analyzes.

This book is a step towards the restoration of Quranic mindset among Muslims. Such a mind understands clearly. It understands the laws of Allah as they manifest in the universe. It focuses on actions that restore the glory in this world and in the sight of God. The glory in this world and the glory in the hereafter are not two separate things: they are meant to go together as the Prophet (S) amply demonstrated.

In this discourse we will present evidence from Quran. All translations of Quran quoted in this book are by Abdullah Yusuf Ali. When we use a different translation, we give the name of the translator in parentheses.

Consider Quran 2:164: "Behold! In the creation of the heavens and the earth; in the alternation of the night and the day; in the sailing of the ships through the ocean for the profit of mankind; in the rain which Allah sends down from the skies and the life which He gives therewith to an earth that is dead; in the beasts of all kinds that He scatters through the earth; in the change of the winds and the clouds which they trail like their slaves between the sky and the earth; (here) indeed are signs for a people that are wise."

Quran clearly asks its readers to be mindful of the phenomena in nature that they experience in their lives. It appeals to your intellect to exercise your wisdom and understand these phenomena, in order to appreciate the truth in Quran, and to get to know Allah. Fact is that this is the best way to get to know Allah.

Appeal to intellect is in response to human desire to achieve glory in this world and also in the hereafter: as is acknowledged in Quran 2:201: "And there are men who say: "Our Lord! give us good in this world and good in the Hereafter and defend us from the torment of the fire!""

This is Quranic exhortation for a mental Hijrah from "taqlid" to wise contemplation; and it is the prescription of Quran to take us out of the mindset created by our experiences during the reign of the dynasties and during the colonial era. We need to migrate to a mindset that Quran clearly prescribes. Prophet (S) brought the verbal descriptions of Quran to life. He produced a society that was glorified in this world and in the eyes of Allah. The guidance embodied in Quran and the Sunnah suggests that the Muslims of today must similarly acquire spiritual emancipation, as well as the position of strength in this world.

The mental Hijrah is a journey of understanding and vision. We need to replace the rigidity of religious doctrines with a focus on purpose. We must base our actions on the clarity of vision and the love of Allah, not on fear and confusion. We must be at peace with ourselves and in harmony with Allah's creation. The peace and harmony are the beginning of spirituality and glory that Allah has promised Muslims.

We need to read Quran, as a book, to understand the guidance embodied in its words. We need to clearly recognize the inspiration that this book offers, and use it to enrich our world-view. We must give up our long-established notions that divide life into religious and secular pursuits. The Prophet freely mixed the two and we must follow that strategy.

There is diversity and richness among people and in their capacity to understand what Quran has for them as a book of guidance. It is highly unlikely that we will all have identical visions arising from our analysis and understanding. This has traditionally been viewed as a problem. It has been resolved by discouraging research and squarely depending on the research performed by folks who lived in a world that has now passed. The notion has given rise to the practice of "taqlid" and the resulting sectarianism has done a profound disservice to Islam and Muslims.

We must check this trend. We need to encourage research. The plurality of understanding is a source of richness rather than a problem. Through our research we contribute to a deeper understanding of Islam and its blessings in the spiritual sense as well as in the secular sense. Our visions provide multiple views of the guidance from Allah and afford us multiple paths for our journey to the promised glory. We must enrich ourselves from the body of research so performed, rather than close our vision behind the curtains of "taqlid".

The Muslims need to make a mental Hijrah towards a Quranic mindset. Such a mind is non-superstitious, makes inquiries, and analyzes the signs of Allah. Quranic mind does not blindly submit to the religious doctrines on one hand and the political authority on the other. It has clear objectives for all actions and a clear vision for all doctrines.

But this will not happen without effort, as is clear from Quran 13:11: "… Verily never will Allah change the condition of a people until they change it themselves …".

A framework is developed in this book in order to facilitate the needed mental Hijrah towards the revival of the Muslim World-View.

1.3 Objectives of Mental Hijrah

The purpose of the mental Hijrah is to achieve the following two objectives, as these are foundational to the Islamic teaching.

1. To build strong, free, and wise individuals with a high degree of Taqwa.

2. The above individuals must constitute a strong, free, and wise Ummah with a high degree of Taqwa in its policies.

Such individuals and such nations can meet Allah with a sense of fulfillment. Taqwa is a Quranic construct. It is the basis for the peace on Earth, a measure for good and bad deeds, the ability to be inspired by Quran, and the closeness with Allah. It is discussed in detail in Theorem 1 on page 129. The Taqwa derives from how successfully one plays one's role in achieving the above two objectives. Please note that Taqwa depends not only on the individual piety, it also requires the role of the individual in the service of Ummah.

In order to achieve these objectives, the following two Quranic requirements are helpful for the framework.

- o The framework seeks to remove sectarianism among Muslims; requiring that the multiplicity of approaches towards an issue be used as an asset. Sectarianism is forbidden as is clear from Quran 3:103: "And hold fast all together by the rope which Allah (stretches out for you) and be not divided among yourselves; ... "

- o The framework seeks to reinforce the worships of Allah in those dimensions that the Muslims have neglected over centuries. These include the worships in the physical dimension and those at the level of the Ummah. These will be discussed in the 'Book of Worships'.

Quran is very explicit about the sources of guidance that the people can use. These sources of guidance are important tools for Muslims to do the Mental Hijrah and develop a correct world-view.

1.4 Allah's guidance

Below we examine the three fundamental sources of guidance. As will be seen in subsequent chapters, Quran prescribes them very clearly. Quran blessed Muslims with these tools, chronologically in the order in which they are listed below, Muslims should deploy them in that order of priority. They must understand these tools and learn to use them.

1.4.1 Human faculties

The first and foremost among the gifts of Allah to the human race is the faculties with which each human being is born. These are a primary resource for a person in living his or her life. Receipt and utilization of any further guidance is based on these primary resources, the use of which is a precondition.

This is made abundantly clear in Quran, even though our Ulama tend to deemphasize it; rather the opposite, our Ulama discourage the use of the human intellect. Human intellect comes from the very act of creation when Allah breathed His Ruh into man, as in Quran 32:9. Lest the mankind would forget, Allah reminded them emphatically in Surah Shams. The first seven Ayahs (91:1-7) are a powerful introduction to what is stated next. In the Ayahs (91:8-10) Allah announces the message to mankind:

"So, I sent an Ilham (enlightenment) to the Soul about its "wrong" and its "right";

Truly, he succeeds who keeps the soul purified;

And he fails who corrupts the soul."

The translation is a slight variation from Yusuf Ali, for clarification. The Surah testifies that Allah has given the needed inspiration to mankind in order for it to decide what is its wrong-doing and what is its right-doing. This inspiration is in the "conscience" of a man. Man can know his conscience through the exercise of intellect; which is, therefore, a primary prerequisite action in order to know the wrong from right. Quran must be understood using this inspiration which therefore, constitutes the primary source for guidance given to mankind by Allah, via His infinite Mercy. We must remember that Allah sends us His Ilham, and we must not be guilty of taking it lightly, or slighting it by not honoring it by refusing to use it.

Without the use of the primary sources, additional guidance cannot be understood and followed. The principal tools included in this primary source of guidance are man's observational and analytical faculties which increase his intellect, and reveal his conscience. Their use is a necessary precondition to understand and follow the further guidance, such as Quran or Sunnah that are described below.

This primary resource is also clearly discussed in Quran elsewhere. It is described as a means through which mankind is better equipped than other creatures such as angels. Quran 32:9: But He fashioned him in due proportion and breathed into him something of His spirit (Ruhi) And He gave you (the faculties of) hearing and sight and feeling (and understanding): little thanks do ye give!"

Using the primary resources mankind can discover knowledge beyond what is available to angels. Quran 2:31: "And He taught Adam the nature of all things; then He placed them before the angels and said: "Tell Me the nature of these if ye are right." The description continues into Quran 15:29 and 38:72: (The two Ayahs read the same) "When I have fashioned him (in due proportion) and breathed into him of My spirit fall ye down in obeisance unto him."

It is a colossal failure of Muslims to not use the primary sources of guidance, and thereby misrepresenting both Quran and Sunnah, the secondary and tertiary sources of guidance.

1.4.2 Quran

Next comes the guidance that Allah sent via His Prophets. This guidance takes the form according to the people to whom it is sent; where it is sent, and when it is sent. Half a millennium before the advent of Quran, the guidance took the form of Injeel, which was different in form from Torah that was sent earlier to the people of Moses in Egypt. For Muslims, this guidance is given in the form of Quran, which format is different from both the Injeel and the Torah.

This guidance is useful only for those who use their primary resources, namely observational and intellectual faculties. While the primary source of guidance is customized for a person, the secondary source is customized for the nation as a whole.

No guidance, even that from Allah Himself, can be of any value for mankind unless it is understood, and then practiced based on that understanding. Such understanding is not possible without the exercise of the primary sources that are built in as part of the act of creation. In His infinite Mercy, Allah built the intellect into the act of creation.

1.4.3 The Sunnah

The acts of the Prophets are also a source of guidance for the human beings. This is because the Prophets are the specially chosen people and possess exceptional insights. The conduct of Mohammad (S) is a source of guidance in this sense. Muslims have therefore taken great pains to report, authenticate, and record the conduct of the Prophet (S).

However, the usefulness of the Sunnah also has preconditions, which are more stringent than those that apply to seeking guidance in Quran. The primary source of intellect must be applied more squarely to seek guidance from the Sunnah. In addition, the guidance in Sunnah is contextual; it is not as general as the guidance in Quran. The biggest limiting factor is that of the space and time; where it happened and when it happened, and under what circumstances. This space and time factor often gets overlooked, thereby giving rise to differences among Muslims, which often take the form of sectarian strife.

1.5   The space-time factors

The mere existence of guidance is not automatically useful. The human observation and intellect must be used to parse this guidance and to visualize the variously many ways in which it can help the individual, the nation, and the nation of nations (the Ummah).

This however is a delicate task. It is neither easy to perform, nor is its outcome fixed. The outcome is, naturally, a function of factors such as the following.

- o   The capacities of the individual or the nation that performs this task,
- o   The format of the guidance itself. The format includes the format of Quran, the Sunnah, and any supplementary information. This changes with space-time. Thus, the format of Quran as used by the early companions of the Prophet was different from how we know it in a compiled book form. Even

after the Caliphs (R) compiled it in a book form, it was not commonly available until the advent of the printing technology. Similarly, the sources of Sunnah today are much different from those available to the early companions of the Prophet. The compilation of the books of Hadith as available to us today, was not available to the well-known four Sunni Imams, as the compilation was in works at that time.

o The framework used to parse the guidance. Such a framework has not existed among Muslims, in any elaborate form. The sects in Islam are based on the opinions of people who developed a following for themselves. This book is an attempt to develop a systematic framework of analysis and decision making that would not be ad hoc and opinion-based.

o The contextual environment of whom, when and where. This functional dependence of the outcome is referred to as the space-time factor. This is the role of the specific circumstances. It enters at two levels. First, the specific circumstances and the contextual details that might be addressed by a particular Quranic revelation or an action of the Prophet. Such Quranic Ayahs and the incidences of the Sunnah need to be understood with Hikmah before application to the situations of today. Second, the situations of today need variables that did not exist within the experience base of the period of Quranic revelation and the life of the Prophet (S). For instance, life is globally interconnected today and will not readily map onto relatively independent states in Medina and Mecca. It is very important in Islamic evaluations to be mindful of the new space-time realities of today. A less than optimum treatment of this aspect can lead to evaluations with suspect applicability.

In his book "Towards an Islamic theory of international relations", second edition, IIIT, 1994, AbdulHamid A. AbuSulayman, in chapter three, describes how Imam Shafi (R) ruled on matters of war and peace. The Imam did not adequately consider the space-time factors. He therefore advised the Muslim rulers to attack the Mushrikun at least once a year, if not more often, and not to accept a truce for more than ten years. Indeed, this opinion is based on the Sunnah of the Prophet, who was engaged with the enemy in a battle at least once a year and accepted a truce for ten years at Hudaibiya. However, such simple-minded analogy and understanding is not acceptable in the context of modern systems of warfare and international relations.

Imam Shafi (R) is not alone with respect to inadequate attention to the space-time factors, and similar examples exist in other matters of Fiqh as well. Therefore, caution is necessary to view the books of Fiqh with a grain of salt.

Out of the three sources of guidance, only one is internal to the human beings: namely the faculties with which the people are born. The other two sources are external; they are proportionately more likely to be misunderstood, and consequently misapplied, as is illustrated in the case of Imam Shafi (R). The guidance from Quran and the conduct of the Prophet must be clearly defined contextually; and it must be unambiguously understood within its prevailing contextual circumstances before it becomes actionable at any given place and at any given time.

In common parlance we speak of "following the guidance". The phrase conjures an image of a road that runs from where you are, to where you want to get to. We expect clearly marked signs at the intersections along the way, helpful signs to keep a safe speed, and informative signs to indicate how far we have traveled.

Each traveler starts her or his journey from a point that is her or his current position in the journey of life. Each one needs to take Quran and Sunnah highway using a different access route, each one drives a different vehicle, each one requires different necessities, and each one reads the roadmaps in a different language. While we talk about "following the guidance", it is not the same straitjacket for everyone.

There is yet another important concept to digest. The guidance must be made actionable at two separate levels. First, the level of the individual; second, the level of the Ummah. Clearly, these two levels of guidance have different requirements, and both are required by Quran and Sunnah.

*

Let us summarize the discussion in this chapter. The Muslim Ummah has been, throughout its existence over the last fourteen centuries, a driving force in the affairs of this World. For most of this duration the Ummah has set the agenda of the World affairs and has made intrinsic contributions to the human emancipation, World peace, and scientific knowledge. It has been about a century that the Muslims have lost their role as a driving force in the World affairs.

This happened because the Muslims made an unfortunate Hijrah from Quranic mindset that enquires and analyzes, to a mindset of blind following without enquiry or comprehension. The remedy to this malady is to revert back to Quranic mindset. This "homecoming" is referred to as the mental Hijrah, which is the first step to revive the Muslim World-View and to restore the torch-bearer role of the Muslim Ummah on this Earth.

Allah has given us guidance for this homeward journey. The first and foremost of His guidance is in the way He created us, for example, with intellectual faculties that help us enquire and analyze. Then He gave us guidance in the form of His book(s). It is incumbent upon us to use the faculties with which Allah created us to comprehend the book of Allah and to use this comprehension to guide our lives as individuals and as an Ummah. This exercise is sensitive to the space-time factors. The Prophet (S) demonstrated, in his own space-time environment, how to use the comprehension of Quran to steer the individual and the Ummah.

2 Solution architecture

In the previous chapter we discussed the Quranic framework of worships in three dimensions, and the problem that the Muslims are facing today because of their neglect towards these worships. We also concluded that the approach to solving this problem involves a mental Hijrah, change in their mindset from Taqlid to thoughtfulness. In this chapter we will present an architecture that will facilitate the needed mental Hijrah. The word architecture is used in the sense of a blue print for further action. It constitutes a Quranic framework in the context of which all other activities are formulated. It is intended to be the beginning of a new era in the lives of Muslims, as individuals, as nations, and as an Ummah.

This architecture derives from Quranic framework of worships in three dimensions. It embodies three important themes that Quran emphasizes. These themes are combined using the overarching principles that Quran provides as the meaning and purpose of these themes. The result is a coherent and forward-looking dynamic architecture. It is intended to take the Muslims back to the position that embodies the spiritual emancipation together with the glory in this world, as is recommended by Quran and practiced by our holy Prophet (S).

The three ingredients of this architecture are the worship of Allah, more worship of Allah, and even more worship of Allah. Indeed, it is made clear in Quran 24:41: "Seest thou not that it is Allah Whose praises all beings in the heavens and on earth do celebrate and the birds (of the air) with wings outspread? Each one knows its own (mode of) prayer and praise. And Allah knows well all that they do".

The word worship is used to represent the teachings of Quran and the act of using them as guidance for everyday life. As we will see, these teachings of Quran are not arbitrary or abstract assertions. They are the divine guidance, each having a well-defined objective. This brings a clear perspective by focusing each worship on the objectives that Quran attributes to that worship. An act detached from its objective loses its dynamic content, and gets reduced to a mere ritual. The purpose behind the act keeps it forward-looking and dynamic. That is the reason Quran describes the acts of worship and binds them to the purpose of each. An immersive reading of Quran will clearly demonstrate this.

This perspective helps the Muslims to move away from the sectarian debates and the ensuing strife. It enables them to act with confidence. Quran provides this confidence, complete with clear milestones and progress-estimation tools. These milestones and tools are invaluable as we travel the road, along the journey of our lives. This journey along the Quranic milestones is indeed the worship of Allah, as Quran tells us.

Quran clearly shows the paths of action for the life of the people. Worship means understanding these paths of action and their objectives, and to carry them out during the voyage of one's life.

Quran prescribes worship in the following three dimensions.

- The dimension of the physical universe
- The dimension of the ethical excellence

o   The dimension of the spiritual emancipation

There is a great wisdom in this Quranic prescription. They take care of the dynamics of life, such that a balanced equilibrium state is attained by observing worships in all three dimensions. On the other hand, the equilibrium and the subtle balance is disturbed if worship in any one of these dimensions is ignored or performed with neglect to its objectives. As we shall see, the worships in one particular dimension cannot help attain the objectives of the worship in a different dimension. Similarly, the performance of the worships in these three dimensions must itself be balanced. Neglecting certain aspects of a worship or an over adherence to it will also cause a loss of equilibrium in life.

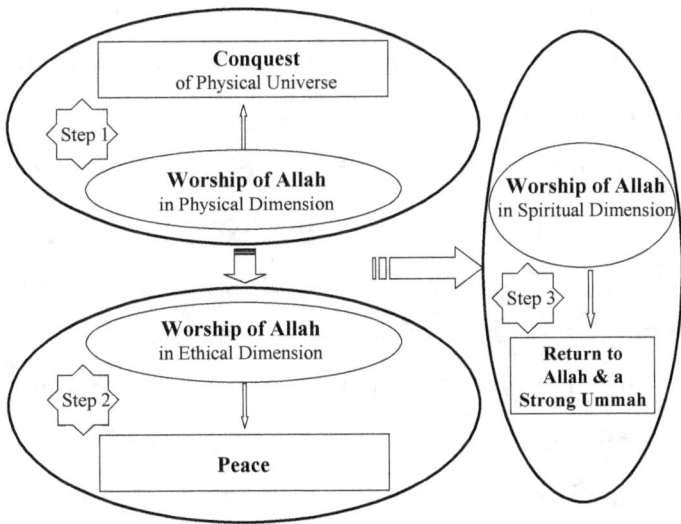

Figure 2–1: Solution architecture based on Quranic framework embedding worships of Allah in three dimensions.

The worships in the three dimensions and the objectives of these worships are schematically shown in figure 2–1. The life of a person is a particular locus in this three-dimensional space. The path one takes through this space determines one's Taqwa These worships constitute the major modules of the architectural framework that we will further elaborate in this book. The three fundamental modules are briefly described below, and further discussed in chapters 3 through 6.

2.1 Worship in the physical dimension

The worships in the physical dimension lead to a deep understanding of the laws of the physical universe, and it affords the conquest of the physical universe to a proportional extent.

We have used the phrase "conquest of the physical universe" in a metaphorical sense, as the physical universe has been made subservient to mankind in Quran 16:12: He has made subject to you the Night and the Day; the Sun and the Moon; and the Stars are in subjection by His Command: verily in this are Signs for men who are wise.

This worship consists of paying attention to the phenomena in the physical universe, as they represent the "signs" of Allah. The deeper we understand the physical phenomena the better we can appreciate the truth in Quran and better we get to know Allah. We must, therefore, observe these "signs" and understand them. This understanding leads to the "conquest" of the physical universe, an aspect that Allah ordained for the mankind though only for those who adequately perform the worship in the physical dimension.

This worship is shown as step 1 in figure 2–1 and it is discussed in greater detail in chapter 3. In a nutshell, this worship is akin to doing research in natural phenomena.

2.2 Worship in the ethical dimension

This worship consists of the dealings of the individual and the society, embracing the inter-personal relationships, the inter-group relationships, and inter-national relationships. The worship consists of observing these relationships with sincerity of intentions.

The sincerity of intentions means a deep and unselfish commitment to the understanding developed via the worships in the physical dimension. This combination of understanding and the commitment leads to Taqwa, as will be further discussed in Theorem 1 on page 129. Just the understanding does not lead to Taqwa, nor does the commitment alone; understanding of nature and commitment in the light of that understanding together constitute Taqwa.

When adequately performed together with the worship in the physical dimension, it leads to the glory in this world. The Sunnah of the Prophet (S) clearly demonstrates how this can be done. Quran guides us to the glory in this world, but also warns us that it is not sought in a secular sense. Unlike the glory sought by an aspiring superpower, it is not an end in itself but a means to an end. It is the means to establish peace on Earth. This is a genuine peace, the purpose of which is to afford all the people the free and nourishing environment, which is generous and sharing and is free from greed and foolishness. All the people of the world deserve such an environment so that everyone and anyone can worship Allah, if they choose to do so. The Muslims have a duty to establish such an environment throughout the world; and when they do so, they fulfill the task of being the Khalifah of Allah on Earth.

This is the inner reflection of the worships in the ethical dimension. This worship is shown as step 2 in figure 2–1 and it is discussed in greater detail in chapter 4.

2.3 Worship in the spiritual dimension

As discussed above, the worships in the physical and ethical dimensions together lead to the Taqwa. The Taqwa is a precondition to perform the worships in the spiritual dimension, in the sense that all spiritual worships must be performed with Taqwa. Thus, the worships in the spiritual dimension are built on the foundation of the worships in the physical and ethical dimensions. The spiritual worship does not carry much credence if it is not based on the worship in physical and ethical dimensions. Such interrelationships between different kinds of worship are of critical importance in producing the right equilibrium in individual life and in the life of a society.

The worships in the spiritual dimension include an aspect that corresponds to the individual and an aspect that corresponds to the community (the Ummah). There is a complicated network of interfaces and feedback mechanisms between these worships. The integrated effect of all these dynamics is the generation of Taqwa and its enhancement. A consequence of Taqwa in the society is the emergence of the Ummah as the World leader in establishing the virtues and purging the evil. Success in life and a fulfilled final return to the Creator is gauged by the extent of one's Taqwa and one's contribution to enhancing the position of the Ummah in the community of nations of the World.

This worship is shown as step 3 in figure 2–1 and it is discussed in greater detail in chapters 5 and 6.

2.4 Discussion of worship

As discussed above, the worship of Allah is performed in three complementary dimensions. Each type of worship has clearly defined objectives. The realization of these objectives accomplishes the spiritual emancipation, which has externally observable manifestations. Through these externally observable manifestations, it is possible to estimate the effectiveness of our efforts.

In parallel with these worships, we represent three steps. These steps are schematically depicted in figure 2–1. They represent a process for performing the three types of worship, so that their interrelationships are correctly observed. This process incorporates the interfaces and feedback loops among the three types of Worship. For example, the contemplation on the physical Ayahs of Allah in Nature helps with the conquest of the physical universe, and also helps generate Taqwa; the worships in the ethical plane reinforce this Taqwa, and helps to achieve peace within oneself, and together with the conquest of the physical universe, achieve peace in the external world. Finally, the spiritual worships with the reinforced Taqwa and peace, enable the individual to prepare for the "return" to Allah, and also the glory of the

Ummah. While the process of worship culminates in the spiritual dimension, it finds its beginning in the physical dimension. The details of this process are interwoven, and discussed in this book.

Quran implies a well-defined interdependence between the role of a person as an individual and as a member of the society (Ummah). The acts of worship that Quran specifies in the three dimensions also have a similar interdependence. The purpose of worship, that an individual performs, is intrinsically coupled with a collective aspect of the society. Thus, no individual should feel that he or she has performed the worship of Allah until the individual feels ever-increasing closeness with Allah as a result of those worships; and the externally observable manifestations of this closeness must be demonstrably visible, at the levels of the individual as well as at the level of the Muslim Ummah. This objective cannot be met through the worship in the spiritual dimension alone. As we shall discuss in chapters 3 and 4 the worships in the physical and ethical dimensions are also essential, and emphatically prescribed in Quran.

We refer to the "Law of Shadows" discussed in Theorem 2 on page 139. Every spiritual worship has a physical manifestation and every physical worship has a spiritual manifestation. Spiritual worship without the corresponding physical shadows is invalid. Spiritual excellence produces physical glory; one cannot exist without the other. This is the litmus test for the validity of all worship, see Quran 13:15: "Whatever beings there are in the heavens and the earth do prostrate themselves to Allah (Acknowledging subjection),- with good-will or in spite of themselves: so do their shadows in the morning and evenings."

*

Let us summarize the discussion in this chapter. Like any human endeavor, the revival of the Muslim world-view requires careful planning, and the execution of the plan. The first milestone in this plan is the needed Mental Hijrah. This is executed using an architectural framework whose modules are the worships of Allah in the three dimensions. It is vital that the Muslims comprehend the meanings, significance, and objectives of each type of worship. Further, they need to understand the interfaces, feedback mechanisms, and the interdependencies between these worships. These considerations are collectively referred to as the architectural framework. The end objective of the architectural framework is to facilitate a successful final return of the individual to Allah, and the emergence of a strong Ummah that can establish righteousness in the World and purge it from evil.

3 Worship in Physical Dimension

This chapter, and the subsequent three chapters, together constitute what we have called the "Book of Worships". Previously, in the 'Book of Framework' we discussed an architectural framework in order to revive the Muslim World-View. That framework consists of three modules, namely the worships of Allah in the physical, ethical, and spiritual dimensions. Those three modules are discussed in detail in this 'Book of Worships'.

The book of worships describes Quranic guidance for physical, ethical, and spiritual activities. These activities constitute the worships of Allah, intended with a grand scheme of overarching themes for the benefit of mankind.

In this book of worships, we will discuss the worships in the three dimensions together with their role in Quranic grand scheme of things.

The present Chapter 3 discusses the worships of Allah in the physical dimension. As we shall see, these worships are akin to performing scientific research, with a twist.

Next Chapter 4 discusses the worships of Allah in the ethical dimension, which addresses the inter-personal conduct, inter-group relationships, and inter-national affairs.

Next Chapters 5 and 6 together describe the worships of Allah in the spiritual dimension: chapter 5 discusses at the individual level, while chapter 6 discusses at the level of Ummah.

*

In the present chapter we start our analysis at the level of the physical dimension. At this level, the discussion is fairly straightforward because the physical dimension is directly observable, and Quranic statements at this level are readily understandable.

There are many Quranic Ayahs that address the physical dimension. They also recommend an attitude that the people should take towards the physical dimension. These Quranic prescriptions are quite explicit. Our objective in this chapter is to understand these Quranic guidelines, focus on their purpose, and make practicable recommendations. These are part of Allah's guidance to all human beings. Additionally, for Muslims they carry the significance of Allah's worship, because they are conducted per Quranic guidance.

Quran addresses the entire human family. This family is the body of children, youth, women, and men who inhabit this Earth. Every one of them has a bond of blood relationship with all others, as in Quran 39:6: "He created you (all) from a single person: then created of like nature his mate; and He sent down for you eight head of cattle in pairs: He makes you in the wombs of your mothers in stages one after another in three veils of darkness. Such is Allah your Lord and Cherisher: to Him belongs (all) dominion. There is no god but He: then how are ye turned away (from your true Center)?". The purpose and the design of Allah with respect to the human family is very profound. As part of this design, Allah bestowed special gifts on all members of this family. It is so, independent of the tribal, national, ethnical, cultural, and religious partitions that exist within the human family.

Let us now explore the guidance that Quran offers in the physical dimension. By definition, following the guidance that Quran offers is an act of worship of Allah. Following Quranic guidance in respect of the physical world constitutes the worships of Allah in the physical dimension.

In this regard, Quran makes very specific instructions that all people must follow. As is always the case, Allah guides mankind, and there are very specific objectives for that guidance. These objectives must always be clearly recognized and understood; otherwise, the guidance of Allah cannot be used objectively.

Before we embark upon the specific worships in the physical dimension, we generally discuss the purpose of those worships. Doing so will help with the big picture in the context of which the individual worships are understood and performed.

Allah promises in Quran that the physical universe is made subservient to mankind. Quran 16:12: "He has made subject to you the Night and the Day; the Sun and the Moon; and the Stars are in subjection by His Command: verily in this are Signs for men who are wise". Further clarification is provided in Quran 14-33: "And has made the sun and the moon, both of them constant upon their courses, subservient [to His laws, so that they be of use] to you; and has made the night and the day subservient [to His laws, so that they be of use] to you." (M. Asad).

The subjection of the physical universe to mankind is gradual, in proportion to the extent that the mankind observes the worships in the physical dimension. In this book we refer to this phenomenon as the

33

gradual "conquest" of the physical universe by mankind. This "conquest of the physical universe" takes place via the understanding of Allah's commands regarding the universe, which is facilitated by the worships in the physical dimension.

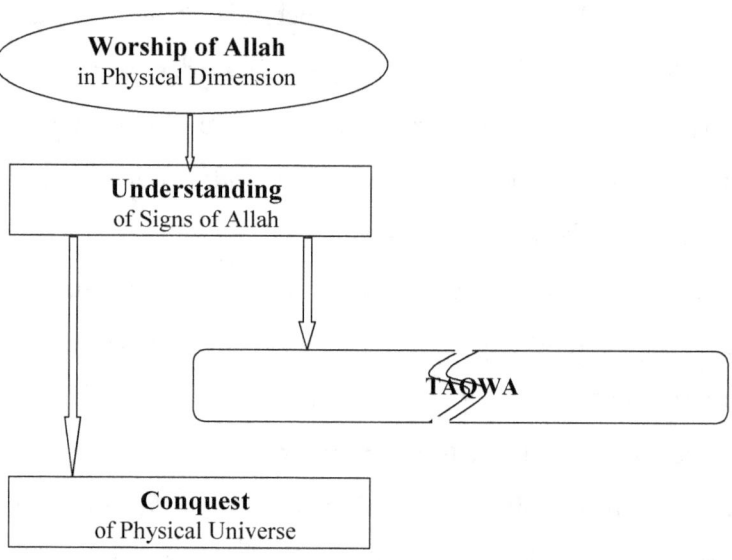

Figure 3-1: The acts of Allah's worship in the "Physical Dimension" lead to the "Conquest" of the physical universe and a component of Taqwa.

The commands of Allah regarding the physical universe are the laws of nature. These laws are manifest in the phenomena of nature; therefore, Quran refers to them as the Ayahs (signs) of Allah.

These laws do not change as stated in Quran 10:64: "… no change can there be in the Words of Allah". This constancy is assured in order to enable the humans towards the "conquest" of the physical universe.

Figure 3-1 schematically illustrates this discussion. The worship of Allah in the physical universe is intended to create a profound understanding of the signs of Allah. This understanding leads to a phenomenon that we called the "conquest of the physical universe".

There is another result of this profound understanding. It forms a component in the equation for the acquisition of Taqwa. The box labeled "Taqwa" is shown sheared in the figure. This is because the understanding alone cannot lead to Taqwa; indeed, it must be complemented by another ingredient, namely a sincere commitment to the understanding, that we will discuss in chapter 4. A detailed discussion of Taqwa is presented in TheoremTheorem 1 1 on page 129.

In the subsections that follow, we will describe some of Quranic worships in the physical dimension.

3.1 Learning

Learning is a very fundamental worship in Islam. It was one of the first instructions that Allah revealed to Mohammad (S). To realize the importance of learning, one must recall that this revelation is addressed to the one who was spiritually most enlightened of all the humanity, Prophet Mohammad (S).

The word used in this revelation is Iqra. Quran 96:1: "Read in the name of thy Sustainer who has created" (M. Asad). Mohammad (S) is the one who was being addressed, and he was the most capable to receive and understand the revelation. He received it and interpreted it to mean the reading of the written word.

What is meant by the written word? It is the expression of the knowledge and the learning. The humans acquire and write down the knowledge for others to read and learn. It also applies to the divine revelation that is written down, for people to read it and learn from it. The discoveries in sciences, humanities, economics, politics, and spirituality etcetera, are similarly written down to be read for the purpose of learning.

Indeed Mohammad (S) acquired all secular knowledge, even though he could not read and write, as was appropriate to his space-time. His close companions did the same. They simultaneously excelled in spirituality and in secular matters. Spiritually speaking, they achieved closeness to Allah that is absolutely exceptional. Secularly speaking, they were the Superpower of the world.

Quranic exhortation for learning is in the sense of general learning, beyond the religious learning. It is a prime religious duty of all Muslims to acquire all the knowledge as is appropriate to their space-time; and to fulfill the two-fold requirement of getting close to Allah and establishing a secular power-base to establish the "good" and abolish the "bad"; we will define these terms latter.

3.2 Observing

The written word is not the only means of learning. It is of course a direct and efficient means to digress what has already been researched. This however is only the beginning of the learning process.

The written word needs to be understood, verified, and further developed with respect to its role in life. Quran prescribes the process of observation for this purpose, Quran 32:27: "Have they not seen how We lead the water to the barren land and therewith bring forth crops whereof their cattle eat, and they themselves? Will they not then see?" Another exhortation for observation is in Quran 3:190: "Behold! in the creation of the heavens and the earth and the alternation of night and day there are indeed Signs for men of understanding."

The process of observation clearly requires the subject being observed. Quran offers the natural phenomenon as things to be observed, Quran 3:190: "Behold! in the creation of the heavens and the earth and the alternation of night and day there are indeed Signs for men of understanding." These signs provide signposts towards Allah. However, there is no simple way to observe and interpret these signs. Different signs point to different attributes of Allah's Laws. A uniform message in these signs is not obvious, and its understanding requires considerable human effort.

Quran exhorts people to discover and learn from these signs, as in Quran 22:46: "Do they not travel through the land so that their hearts (and mind) may thus learn wisdom and their ears may thus learn to hear?" The signs point to the laws of nature, which represent Allah's commandments, as is stated in Quran 2:117: "To Him is due the primal origin of the heavens and the earth; when He decreeth a matter He saith to it: "Be"; and it is". Man gets to know these commandments as the laws of nature. As discussed earlier, Allah's commands do not change, which lends a degree of permanence to the laws of nature. These laws are themselves signs of Allah as they fulfill their role in Allah's design for creation.

Everything in the universe praises the glory of Allah, as in Quran 17:44: "The seven heavens and the earth and all beings therein declare His glory: there not a thing but celebrates His praise; and yet ye understand not how they declare His glory!" Through the discovery of the laws of nature Mankind too can get to know the glory of Allah. This happens via the worships of Allah in the physical dimension, which reveal the mysteries of the signs of Allah and lead one to Him.

The process of this discovery embeds within it the processes of the scientific research. This research is part of the learning process and is an act of worship.

The struggle of Ibrahim (A) is an example of this discovery process, indicated in Quran 6:74-79:

"Lo! Abraham said to his father Azar: "Takest thou idols for gods? for I see thee and thy people in manifest error."

So also did We show Abraham the power and the **laws of the heavens and the earth** that he might (with understanding) have certitude.

When the night covered him over he saw a star: he said: "this is my Lord." But when it set he said: "I love not those that set."

When he saw the moon rising in splendor He said: "This is my Lord." but when the moon set he said: "Unless my Lord guide me I shall surely be among those who go astray."

When he saw the sun rising in splendor he said: "This is my Lord; this is the greatest (of all)." But when the sun set he said: "O my people! I am (now) free from your (guilt) of giving partners to Allah.

"For me I have set my face firmly and truly toward Him Who created the heavens and the earth, and never shall I give partners to Allah."

This demonstrates how the research into the natural phenomena (stars, moon, sun) points towards Allah. While it is acceptable to make honest mistakes in the course of this struggle, not to struggle in this direction is a clear disregard for Allah's guidance.

Compliance with this guidance provides mankind the power of knowledge acquired through research, as in Quran 55:33: "O ye assembly of Jinns and men! if it be ye can pass beyond the zones of the heavens and the earth pass ye! not without authority shall ye be able to pass!" This power is vital for the conquest of the universe. It does not come without performing the worships in the physical dimension that Quran prescribes; they embed the scientific research within them.

Conquest of universe will come only through worships in the physical dimension, irrespective of what other worships are performed in ethical and spiritual dimensions. All forms of worship have their intended goals. Lack of one form cannot be compensated by attention to another.

3.3 Understanding

Quran clearly emphasizes phenomena are the "signs" of Allah; they are an aid towards knowing Allah. In Quranic parlance, this knowledge of Allah is referred to as "Iman in Allah". However, this comes only after a deep understanding of the "signs" of Allah. This depth of understanding can also bring a deeper Iman in Allah.

Understanding is the purpose behind the acts of reading, learning, and observation: it is like developing a theory based on the observations, in the light of the accumulated knowledge written down by mankind. Quran exhorts people to develop such an understanding, via the exercise of wisdom, as was discussed above.

Quranic prescription goes beyond reading, observing, and theorizing. It requires the people to be in the "know" of the natural phenomenon. As stated in Quran 6:75: "So also did We show Abraham the power and the laws of the heavens and the earth that he might (with understanding) have certitude".

To be in the "know" of the "Ayahs" of Allah produces certitude.

People should not be content with superficial observations and theories that they hold as dogmas, without seeking verification and validation. This was sometimes the case in Greek philosophies. For example, Aristotle taught that speed of fall under gravity is proportional to the weight of the falling object. The dogma was held for nearly two millennia! Galileo Galilei (born February 15, 1564) is reported to have shown the error of this dogma by dropping two objects of different weight simultaneously, and demonstrating that they arrive on earth simultaneously. The established dogmas are not easy to challenge, as in our times is the dogma of sectarianism among the four Madhhabs. Galileo paid for challenging a dogma when his contract with the university of Pisa was not renewed. But this was only the beginning of his punishment. A Florentine priest denounced Galilei from the pulpit because Galileo held that interpretation of the

Bible should be adapted to increasing knowledge and that no scientific position should be made an article of Christian faith.

The Jesuit cardinal Robert Bellarmine instructed Galileo that he must no longer hold or defend his concept that the earth moves. Galileo was summoned to Rome by the Inquisition to stand trial for "grave suspicion of heresy". Galileo was sentenced to life imprisonment. His *book* was ordered to be burned, and the sentence against him was to be read publicly in every university. Galileo became blind and he died at Arcetri, near Florence, on January 8, 1642. In October 1992 a papal commission acknowledged the Vatican's error.

Quran requires that the people keep an open mind and continue the acts of worship with respect to reading, observing, and understanding until they are in the "know" of the things, as in Quran 17:36: "Follow not that whereof thou hast no knowledge. Lo! the hearing and the sight and the heart - of each of these it will be asked".

This of course is an ongoing process because no human understanding (including the human understanding of Quran) and no human theory (including the theory of Fiqh) can be ever final.

There is a more profound aspect to this insistence of Quran on knowledge and certitude. This is the threshold at which the human existence is ready to make the next leap. This leap is to "internalize" the knowledge that the humans gain with their research. This leap is not the leap of the blind faith but the leap of "profound knowledge and certitude". The scientific research helps a person to integrate the experience of knowledge. The more profoundly we understand the

41

Ayahs of Allah, the more clearly we see Allah in the core of our existence.

3.4 Worship and Science

If one examines the acts of worship discussed in this chapter, one cannot fail to see an unmistakably compelling parallel that these Quranic prescriptions have with the methodology of scientific research. This parallel is obvious in this space-time at the dawn of the 21st century. However, this parallel did not exist at the time of Quranic revelations. The methodology of scientific research was not yet well developed and widely accepted. Quranic guidelines were decisively ahead of the times.

In this respect it is important to observe that Quran uses the term "Ayah" in a dual sense. Sometimes they refer to the natural phenomena. Sometimes they refer to the verbal statements and declarations in Quran. This is very profound. In adopting this approach Quran explicitly acknowledges the intrinsic identity between the verbal Quran and the book of nature that everyone can internalize via the prescription of reading, observing, understanding, and knowing. No dichotomy can ever be found between these two versions of the book of Allah. This is the profoundest proof of the divine origin of Quran.

3.5 Research and Muslims

Quranic guidance in the physical dimension is universal. Whoever will heed it will see the reward. One does not need to be a Muslim, Hindu, Christian, Budh, Jew, or Pagan. Anyone can practice the prescription and reap the reward. Many people over the course of history have paid heed to these principles and seen their reward, such as the Euro-American people in the current time. The principles themselves are completely determined by Allah, as in Quran 36:82: "Verily when He intends a thing His command is "Be" and it is!" People can seek the discovery of the "commands" of Allah using many source. The source can be the human perseverance in research, it can be the written word by scholars, and it can also be via a divine inspiration. The rules are firmly laid out by the creator of the universe, and they are, by design, discoverable to enable the "conquest of the universe" by mankind.

Quran has incorporated the guidance for these discoveries. The early Muslims, in the 7th through 17th centuries heeded this guidance and they established the foundations of the sciences, as well as expanded their frontiers. The pioneering works of these Muslim scientists enabled Renaissance in Europe. Yet the Muslims today do not use it to excel towards the "conquest" of the universe. The question arises, as to why this turned out to be so? This was despite the teachings of Quran that not only encourage but also require such research. The disregard towards research that is prevalent among the Muslims of today is clearly not part of Islam. This un-Islamic behavior was introduced and firmly planted among Muslims by the later day Ulama, because of the malice of colonialism and neo-colonialism. The term Ulama is used here to collectively refer to the sincere and well-intentioned scholars of Islamic ideology. They developed a substantial popular following for themselves: however, they nevertheless erred in some of their opinions, especially with regard to paying due attention

43

to the space-time factors, and specifically to the Quranic prescriptions for scientific research. This rise and fall of civilizations is a general phenomenon in human history; it is not intended as a criticism of Ulama, even if they unknowingly became instruments of Islamic decay.

Quran has given us the guidance. The meanings and the purpose of this guidance was however changed by the Ulama. This change was in two essential ways. First, they restricted the significance of "learning" to the study of Quran, the Hadith and the Fiqh. This restriction was misleading, because these specific books did not even exist at the time of the Quranic revelations. Second, they went farther along the direction of the deviation from Quranic intent with respect to "learning". They changed the meaning of "reading" Quran from the connotation of learning and understanding to merely producing the sounds for Quranic Ayahs in Arabic.

One requirement for the mental Hijrah that Muslims so badly need is to rectify this grave and fatal error. Muslims must embrace all knowledge wherever they can find it. They must not merely embrace knowledge; they must actually excel in it and produce it through research.

While Muslims must excel in scientific research, it is clearly not required that every individual becomes an accomplished scientist in a professional sense because the worships in the physical dimension are mandatory for a Muslim community (Kifayah). However, it is a Quranic requirement that all Muslims must have an open mind and possess a scientific attitude. This Quranic attitude is part of the

Muslim World-View, and it requires a willingness to learn, make impartial observations, and exercise the natural intellectual reasoning skills.

In addition, the Muslim nations as the Ummah must have accomplished scientists that excel in research and discovery. If scientific attitudes do not exist in the Muslim public or the nation does not possess research excellence, then it is clear that Quranic requirement has been disregarded and nation as a whole has failed in performing a fundamental worship.

3.6 A caution

Some people might argue that Quranic prescription is an invitation to use the observations and understanding of the "signs" of Allah in order to develop a Iman in Allah. They might argue that the need for these activities ends or substantially diminishes once a person declares his or her Iman in Allah.

This is a false line of reasoning that violates the purpose behind this Quranic guidance. The Iman in Allah is not a binary entity that either exists or does not exist. It is a traversal of a huge continuum, as will be discussed in greater detail in the next section. Just because a person declares Iman in Allah does not terminate that person's struggle to know and love Allah. In fact, the verbal declaration is often just the beginning of this pursuit.

Even the most accomplished Muslims have had to traverse stages of Iman in Allah. The case of Ibrahim (A) is a good illustration; as in Quran 2:260: "Behold! Abraham said: "My Lord! show me how thou givest life to the dead". He said: "Dost thou not then believe?" He said: "Yea! but to satisfy my own understanding." He said: "Take four birds; tame them to turn to thee; put a portion of them on every hill and call to them; they will come to thee (flying) with speed. Then know that Allah is Exalted in Power Wise.""

Please note that Ibrahim (A) had this lack of certainty despite Allah's statement that He gave Ibrahim (A) certitude. It is significant to note that when Ibrahim (A) begged Allah in order to satisfy the feeling in his heart, Allah chose to provide the requested satisfaction via a manifest experimental demonstration versus a deep religious discourse. Experimentation indeed is paramount.

All human beings are of course not in the lucky position of Ibrahim (A). They nevertheless do have a greater need to experience the manifest demonstration of the "signs" of Allah in order to formulate and strengthen their "Taqwa". This is amply facilitated by a continued struggle to read, observe, understand, and know the natural phenomena. This is scientific research, an essential and primary form of worship in the physical dimension.

*

Let us summarize the discussion in this chapter. Allah has prescribed certain attitudes and practices that all people must inculcate and practice to achieve the "conquest of the universe". These include the acquisition of knowledge about the physical phenomenon. Reading, observing, theorizing are some of the tools that Quran offers for acquiring a profound knowledge. As prescriptions of Allah revealed abundantly in Quran, these are worships of Allah that are obligatory.

They are obligatory to the extent that they will lead to the conquest of the physical universe on one hand, and as will be discussed in the next chapter, they will produce "certitude" in one's Iman as well as help in the establishment of peace on Earth.

As is generally the case, there is a penalty for disregarding these worships. The penalty for disregarding the worships in the physical dimension is twofold. First, those who abandon these worships shall not conquer the physical universe. Second, and this will be discussed in the next chapter; those who abandon these worships shall not be the ones whose way of life shall flourish on Earth.

4 Worship in ethical dimension

The discussion in Chapter 3 was in the physical dimension. In this section we will go beyond the physical dimension and include some rudimentary aspects of spirituality in our discussion.

The minimum level of spirituality is the ethics. This is a small spiritual step, though a necessary one, towards fuller spirituality. However, even a rudimentary level of spirituality, namely worships in ethical dimension, can be adequate for achieving the goal of "peace". Peace cannot be achieved just based on the worships in the physical dimension, as the world events have already made obvious by now. It is magical, but adding worships in the ethical dimension will make peace minimally possible; it is the threshold of peace on earth.

For this purpose, mankind needs to move beyond the mere acquisition of powers via the "conquest" of the universe. They must become ethical beings. These ethics are intended to guide the relationships between the individuals, the communities, and the nations.

4.1 The worships

The worships in the physical dimension afford the mankind the conquest of the physical universe. This places such powers in the human hands as are fit for deities. Yet the humans are apt to use them with foolishness and greed. This assures the self-destruction of mankind unless the foolishness and greed give way to a focus on selfless service. This is the role of the worships in the ethical dimension.

Quran describes some fundamental principals in the ethical dimension. Quran 24:55: "Allah has promised to those among you who believe and work righteous deeds that He will of a surety grant them in the land inheritance (of power) as He granted it to those before them; that He will establish in authority their religion the one which He has chosen for them; and that He will change (their state) after the fear in which they (lived) to one of security and peace:"

Quran thus makes a promise to mankind. This promise states that the following.

IF

The people Believe and perform Righteously;

Then

Allah will

Give them "khilafah" on the Earth,

Their way of life will flourish, and

They will enjoy "peace".

In this chapter we will explore the meanings of Khilafah and Iman (Taqwa); the technical terms that Quran has used to make the above covenant with mankind. We will then go into the details of worships in ethical dimension.

Figure 4-1 schematically illustrates the linkage between the worships in the ethical dimension and the peace on Earth, as promised by Quran. Figure 4-1 should be studied together with Figure 3-1.

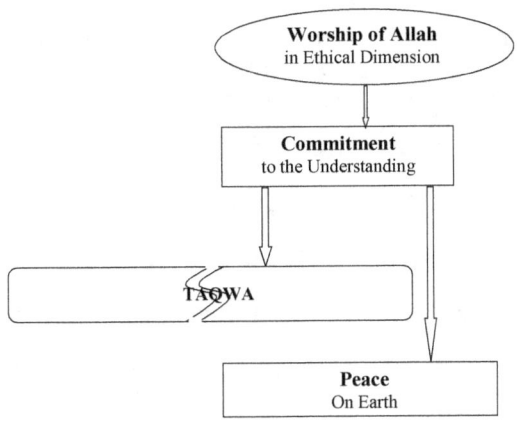

Figure 4-1: Allah's worship in the Ethical dimension results in "Peace" on Earth when combined with the "conquest" of the physical universe, and it also generates a component of Taqwa.

The worships in the physical dimension, as discussed in chapter 3, produce a profound understanding of the signs of Allah. The worships in the ethical dimension that we will discuss in this chapter produce an unselfish commitment to that understanding. This unselfish commitment is a component of the equation that generates Taqwa. The box labeled "Taqwa" is shown sheared in the figure. This is because the unselfish commitment alone cannot lead to Taqwa; indeed, it must be complemented by the profound understanding as was discuss in chapter 3. A detailed discussion of Taqwa is presented in Theorem 1 on page 129. The worships in the physical and ethical dimensions, and the Taqwa that derives from them, all together lead to Peace on Earth, when coupled with the "conquest" of the physical universe.

The dynamics are controlled by Taqwa which derives from the understanding obtained from the worship in the physical dimension plus the commitment that derives from the worship in the ethical dimension. The Taqwa that is thus obtained is minimally sufficient to obtain peace on earth: peace for everybody, not just for the strong.

We will see in the next Chapter 5 that addition of worships in the spiritual dimension will make this fledgling peace into a peaceful paradise.

4.2 Khalifah on earth

Quran describes the creation of Adam. The description is repeated in multiple contexts owing to its fundamental significance.

Quran 2:30-34

"Behold thy Lord said to the angels: "I will create a vicegerent on earth." They said "Wilt thou place therein one who will make mischief therein and shed blood? Whilst we do celebrate Thy praises and glorify Thy holy (name)?" He said: "I know what ye know not."

And He taught Adam the nature of all things; then He placed them before the angels and said: "Tell Me the nature of these if ye are right. "They said: "Glory to Thee of knowledge we have none save that Thou hast taught us: in truth it is Thou who art perfect in knowledge and wisdom."

He said: "O Adam! tell them their natures." When he had told them Allah said: "Did I not tell you that I know the secrets of heaven and earth and I know what ye reveal and what ye conceal?"

And behold We said to the angels: "Bow down to Adam"; and they bowed down not so Iblis he refused and was haughty he was of those who reject Faith."

The description is in parables that can be understood in more ways than one. Allah decided to create a Khalifah on Earth who would act on His behalf. He disclosed this intention to the Angels. Their first response was the feeling that they worshipped Allah adequately. They further felt that the creation of a Khalifah might lead to disruption and bloodshed. Allah told the Angels that He possesses such knowledge, as the Angels do not.

Allah taught Adam the names of all the things. This obviously is a parable. Adam was not merely given the "names" of all the things, but Allah gave Adam the fundamental ingredients to acquire the knowledge about all things. After giving Adam this special knowledge, Allah demonstrated the superiority of Adam's knowledge over that of the Angels (knowledge is indeed a discriminating factor in Islam; according to some traditions, Quranic revelation started with the word "Read", which is a means of acquiring knowledge). They submitted to Allah praising Him and admitting their ignorance in this matter.

Allah asked the Angels to bow down to Adam. The Angels complied with the exception of Iblis, the Shaitan. Indeed, Iblis showed arrogance and he refused to admit a manifest truth that had been clearly demonstrated without a shadow of doubt. Thus, Iblis is called a Kafir, someone who recognizes a manifest truth in his or her conscience and yet refutes it because of pride and arrogance. (The very nature of Kufr means that no other human being can detect it or know it. Only Allah knows it. Of course, the person committing the act of Kufr also knows it, because he knows when he is violating the call of the conscience out of ulterior motives.)

This description brings forward at least two important points. First is the fact that mankind was created as the "Khalifah" on Earth. Second, Allah prepared the mankind for this task, and gave them the means to learn all the things pertaining to this world.

4.3 Taqwa and Iman

As was discussed above, Taqwa is a composition of two ingredients.

1. The profound understanding that is gained from the signs of Allah, as was discussed in chapter 3, Worship in Physical Dimension.

2. A total commitment (submission) to this understanding, that derives from the worships in the ethical dimension as is discussed in this chapter.

The details are discussed in Theorem 1 on page 129.

The second component of Taqwa (i.e., the total commitment) is referred to as the Iman in Quranic terminology. Quran often uses the term Iman in two different senses. One is as described above, in the sense of a total commitment. The second is in the context of describing the articles of Iman, e.g., describing the Iman in Allah, the books, the prophets, the Angels, and the day of Judgement. These latter articles will be discussed in chapter 5.

One might wonder what Quran calls as the righteous deeds, or good deeds. These are deeds performed with Iman with the intention of doing good. The word "good" is understood in the context of the society where such deeds are performed, when they are performed.

Please note that the translators use the terms faith and belief though Quran has no such terminology, preferring to only use the term Iman which means knowing. The translators use the Christian terms like faith and belief in place of the term Iman, thereby corrupting the message of Quran with Christian conceptual innovations.

Taqwa is a Quranic construct that includes the concept of total commitment (Iman) and profound understanding (Wisdom). It is therefore more comprehensive than either one of its two components. Quran therefore uses Taqwa as the precondition to be able to derive guidance from the book, as well as the final criterion of the spiritual emancipation, as will be discussed in Theorem 1 on page 129.

Worships in the ethical dimension are the righteous deeds that Quran requires together with the Taqwa. If righteous deeds are performed and a level of Taqwa is maintained, then Allah's promise can be realized. This promise allows the people in question to become Khalifah on Earth by inheriting the secular power. We refer to it as "secular" in the sense that it derives solely from the worships in the physical and ethical dimensions. The promise also allows the establishment of peace, under their way of life, those who acquire this power.

Quran clearly states that one purpose of this revealed book is to guide mankind. If the mankind sincerely seeks the paths towards peace, maintaining a level of Taqwa, Allah guides them on these paths, as in Quran 5:16: "Wherewith Allah guideth all who seek His good pleasure to ways of peace and safety and leadeth them out of darkness by His Will unto the light guideth them to a Path that is Straight". Indeed, Allah calls towards the abode of peace and offers His guidance for those who seek it, as in Quran 10:25: "And [know that] God invites [man] unto the abode of peace, and guides him that wills [to be guided] onto a straight path" (M. Asad).

The theme of peace runs constant in Quran. It is loud and clear in this world, as in Quran 36:58: "peace and fulfillment through the word of a Sustainer who dispenses all grace" (M. Asad); and it is loud and clear in the Paradise, as in Quran 56:26: "but only the tidings of an inner soundness and peace" (M. Asad).

The subsections that follow provide the details of the worship in the ethical dimension. These are the righteous deeds as Quran elaborates them for all mankind. These worships, performed with Taqwa, lead to the establishment of peace.

Worships in the ethical dimension are discussed in the sections below.

4.4 The individual ethics

Quran provides ethical guidance at the individual level as well as at the level of the society. In this section we will focus on Quranic guidance for individuals.

In evaluating the efficacy of the worships in the ethical dimension, Quran is not interested merely in the physical actions of the individual. It is equally interested in the frame of mind behind those actions. This coupling between the physical actions and the intent behind them is intrinsic, and it derives as a corollary to the very concept of Taqwa.

The following subsections describe some of the worships that Quran prescribes in the ethical dimension. As stated earlier, these are at the level of the individuals.

4.4.1 The causality

Quran uses the concept of self-policing with respect to the sincere observance of the "worship". It means that no external enforcement mechanism is needed at the individual level. The concept uses a philosophical framework where the individual desires to perform the worship out of a profound understanding of the nature of worship, the need for compliance, and the consequences of the failure to comply.

The sincerity of the actions and the intent behind them is clearly articulated by Quran, using the concept of strict causality. It emphasizes that there is no thought or action, no matter how small, that is without consequences, as in Quran 31-16: ""O my son!" (said Luqman) "If there be (but) the weight of a mustard-seed and it were (hidden) in a rock or (anywhere) in the heavens or on earth Allah will bring it forth: for Allah understands the finest mysteries (and) is well-acquainted (with them)". Quran explicitly asserts that there will be an accounting for even an atom worth of good deed and an atom worth of bad deed, as in Quran 99:7-8: "Then shall anyone who has done an atom's weight if good, see it. And anyone who has done an atom's weight of evil, shall see it."

This approach is a fine expression of causality. Every human action produces result, such that the results of human actions become inescapable. The reverse is also true, namely, every human result is the outcome of an effort that causes it, as in Quran 53:39: "That man can have nothing but what he strives for."

The causality is expressed purely in terms of the physical actions and their results. The mechanisms that support and enforce the causality are not discussed at this stage. Some insight will be provided in Chapter 5, using the spiritual dimension.

The causality constitutes the foundation for the sincere implementation of all worship, and is itself a worship. This concept is so powerful that most Muslims, even those who are otherwise lax in their practices, strongly subscribe to its implications.

4.4.2 Balance and justice

Quran asks people to know the balance that exists in nature, as in Quran 30:30: "and so, set thy face steadfastly towards the [one ever-true] faith, turning away from all that is false, in accordance with the natural disposition which God has instilled into man; [for,] not to allow any change to corrupt what God has thus created – this is the [purpose of the one] ever-true faith; but most people know it not" [M. Asad].

The mankind should get inspiration from this balance. This inspiration should guide them to adopt a balanced concept of justice. Once adopted the balance and the justice should be respected, as in Quran 59:9: "So establish weight with justice and fall not short in the balance". This emphasis on balance and justice holds firm in all that a person thinks or acts.

This notion towards the balance and the justice has at least two aspects. One is in the compliance of it; and the other is in the violation of it. Both are a function of the philosophical frame of mind of the individual. The compliance is with an inspiration to respect nature with the explicit understanding that the humans are a part of nature. The violation of these laws is to be viewed as activities that spoil the balance in nature including the balance between humans and the rest of nature.

The act of understanding this balance and observing it is an ethical worship. The violation of the natural concepts of balance and justice can be seen in the so called "Global Climate Warming" due to the anthropogenic activities associated with some economic and industrial processes and the disposal of their waste.

4.4.3 Human respect and dignity

Quran has a subtle way of promoting respect for the individual and the human dignity. For this purpose, it uses the very foundation for the continuation of the human species, namely the inter relations between the parents and children. Ensuring the human respect and dignity for the parents, transitively extends it to practically all the mankind.

Quran has very explicit guidelines in this regard, as in Quran 31:14: "And We have enjoined on man (to be good) to his parents: in travail upon travail did his mother bear him and in years twain was his weaning: (hear the command) "Show gratitude to Me and to thy parents:

to Me is (thy final) Goal"". People generally experience both roles in their lives; the children of today are the parents of tomorrow. Quran thus includes the entire mankind when it defines a loving and kind relationship between the parents and the children.

Please note how Quran regards observance of this respect and dignity at a level comparable to the obedience to Allah. However, the obedience to Allah takes precedence in a situation that produces a conflict between the obedience to Allah and the obedience to parents.

This is a profound expression of respect for the individual and dignity of mankind. Quran accomplishes it by making the statement "Show gratitude to Me and to thy parents: to Me is (thy final) Goal". The gratitude to humans is being stated in the same breath as the gratitude to Allah. The statement is not merely rhetoric, because Quran intends it as it intends "worship" of Allah: being careful to make the guidance precise by resolving any conflicts of allegiance.

The plight of the senior citizens is so sad in the presence of such explicit and high priority guidance, and worship in the ethical dimension. In this light it is indeed not comforting to observe that so many Muslims do not treat their parents as they should. Such a failure of Muslims in performing "worship" in the ethical dimension is a serious shortcoming. It is a direct disobedience of the command of Allah, and it cannot be compensated by the observance of the five pillars of Islam. The five pillars are in a different dimension from the ethical dimension, and worship in each dimension must be independently performed.

4.4.4 Good deeds

Quran makes it abundantly clear that good deeds performed with "Iman" are the only way out of the bad predicament in which people often find themselves. Quran devotes a small Surah entirely to this theme, Quran 103: "By (the Token of) time (through the Ages). Verily Man is in loss. Except such as have Faith and do righteous deeds and (join together) in the mutual teaching of Truth and of Patience and Constancy".

The Iman is related to Taqwa, which is the foundation for the righteous deeds, since without it there would be no meaningful definition of what a righteous deed is. Further, there would be no measure of the sincerity of commitment that is behind the righteous deed. Therefore, Quran asserts an inalienable coupling between the Iman and a righteous deed. The Iman is the foundation for the righteous deeds, and the righteous deeds are an external manifestation of the Iman.

Next comes the purpose of the good deeds; namely, to join forces with all those who know (have Iman in) the truth to uphold the truth. It ascribes a collective meaning to the concept of the righteous deeds. Thus, the righteous deeds, the truth, and upholding the truth are concepts that must have collective meaning. Since the individuals in a society are likely to have differing understanding of these concepts, therefore, it is incumbent upon the individuals to keep their understanding sufficiently flexible so that they can meaningfully cooperate with others to uphold the truth. A rigid understanding on the part of the individuals would make such cooperation difficult and thus defeat

61

the collective objective of the society that Quran prescribes. Quran categorically disallows such rigidity, and it clearly favors a collective effort that is free from sectarianism and partisanship, as in Quran 3:103: "And hold fast all together by the rope which Allah (stretches out for you) and be not divided among yourselves; ..."

The Surah next indicates a process to uphold the truth. The process is based on the exercise of patience and perseverance. It means that the person performing the righteous deeds must also demonstrate patience in whatever sense and context it may be needed.

A similar guidance is expressed in Quran as coming from a wise man, Quran 31-17: "O my son! establish regular prayer enjoin what is just and forbid what is wrong: and bear with patient constancy whatever betide thee; for this is firmness (of purpose) in (the conduct of) affairs".

4.4.5 Bad deeds

Quran also spells out deeds that are not good, Quran 7:33: "Say: The things that my Lord hath indeed forbidden are: shameful deeds whether open or secret; sins and trespasses against truth or reason; assigning of partners to Allah for which he hath given no authority; and saying things about Allah of which ye have no knowledge". They too carry a collective meaning in the context of the society. They include actions that are regarded as shameful or sinful, actions that transgress, to entertain doctrines for which there exists no clear evidence and to practice ideas that are not based on knowledge and understanding. Quran provides the principals under which deeds can be evaluated to be bad. They include all deeds that go against a manifest truth, acts that are not based on manifest evidence, and acts that are not based on a sound understanding.

4.5 Society and the individual ethics

Society is composed of individuals. There is no sharp line as to when the role of the individual with respect to the society begins. The ethical worships discussed earlier apply also to the role of the individual in the society. In this section we discuss additional acts of ethical worship that specifically focus on the role of the individual in the society.

Quran makes it absolutely clear that the acts of worship are solely for the benefits of the individual worshipper and the society that collectively adheres to them. Allah has no benefit to derive from these worships, Quran 10:108: "Say: "O ye men! now Truth hath reached you from your Lord! Those who receive guidance do so for the good of their own souls; those who stray do so to their own loss: and I am not (set) over you to arrange your affairs"".

There are few important departures to note here with respect to other religious notions that prevailed. Quran makes it absolutely irrelevant to have to make sacrifices focused towards pleasing deities for the purpose of avoiding some hardships. Quran presents a physical world that is causal (see previous section), and offers worships that are for the benefit of mankind alone.

So, Quran makes no demand on the humans through the "worships" at the physical or ethical levels, except that these worships are necessary preconditions for "conquering" the physical universe and acquiring "Peace" on Earth.

This is an important departure from the conventional religious practices. It disallows any dogmas that can be enforced under religious doctrines.

Below we describe additional worships in the ethical dimension that apply at the level of the society.

4.5.1 No discrimination

Quran requires that the society treat all people equally. No value can be based on unrealistic considerations like those of race, color, and ethnicity, etc. Quran makes these aspects irrelevant by proclaiming that all humans have the same origin, Quran 49-13: "O mankind! We created you from a single (pair) of a male and a female and made you into nations and tribes that ye may know each other (not that ye may despise each other). Verily the most honored of you in the sight of Allah is (he who is) the most righteous of you... ".

There is one and only one criterion of excellence. It is based on one's Taqwa and one's deeds (see sections 4.3, 4.4.4 and 4.4.5).

4.5.2 Do not disrupt peace

Quran recognizes that some folks would be influenced by peripheral considerations and cause disruption in the world. This is manifestly prohibited. The prohibition must be observed just like a religious worship.

Some folks would take differing postures depending upon their disposition. In austere times they may take a humble posture and be heedful to the worships that are for the benefit of mankind. However, their Iman is not of excellent degree and they are overtaken by greed when the austerity passes, Quran 10:23: "But when He delivereth them Behold! they transgress insolently through the earth in defiance of right! O mankind! your insolence is against your own souls an enjoyment of the life of the Present: in the end to Us is your return and We shall show you the truth of all that ye did". They do not mind causing disruption in opposition to what is right. When they are reminded of this transgression, they respond with pretensions, Quran 2: 11: "When it is said to them: "Make not mischief on the earth" they say: "Why we only want to make peace!"". When they are asked to join the righteous attitudes, they equate the righteousness with foolishness, Quran 2:13: "When it is said to them: "Believe as the others believe" they say: "Shall we believe as the fools believe?" nay of a surety they are the fools but they do not know"".

4.6 The peace

The ethical worships discussed in this chapter are necessary for achieving peace on Earth. There are other ethical worships that Quran also prescribes, so that the set of worships that I have described is not exhaustive. However, to the extent that the set may serve as almost complete, the ethical worships discussed in this chapter are proportionately sufficient conditions to achieve the peace on Earth.

The peace that Quran promises is not an uneasy peace, or a peace under the force of a superpower. The peace that these ethical worships bring to the entire mankind is a genuine peace where the members of the human family actually feel that they have the blessings of peace.

At this stage, let us revisit the worships in the physical and ethical dimensions. These were discussed in chapter 3 and in the current chapter. Their interrelationship was discussed in section 4.3 and illustrated in figure 4-1. Following points may be recalled.

- o The peace on Earth requires Taqwa as well as the acts of worship in the ethical dimension.

- o The acts of worship in the physical dimension can lead to the development of Taqwa in an individual, though this is not automatic; the individual needs some ethics as well. The acts of worship in the physical dimension are required for the peace on Earth in as much as they contribute to the creation of Taqwa.

- o The acts of worship in the physical dimension are required for the conquest of the physical universe. Iman is not required for this conquest. Power without Iman creates a dangerous situation because it places immense powers in potentially dangerous hands.

Quran informs us of people whose Iman may be lacking (see previous section). These people can be apt to disrupt peace at small and a large scale. Therefore, in the absence of Iman, the conquest of the physical universe places dangerous means in careless hands. This poses a serious possibility of anarchy and bloodshed, as was originally expressed by the Angels (see section 4.2). It then becomes mandatory for the people with Iman to also accomplish the conquest of the physical universe in order to provide the capability to deter mischief and bloodshed.

5 Worship in Spiritual Dimension: Individual Perspective

In this chapter we discuss some spiritual aspects that go beyond the ethical dimension.

First, let us clarify a possible misunderstanding. The layout of the chapters for the three forms of worship in this book as well as the corresponding three steps displayed in the architectural figure 2–1 must not be understood to imply a sequence or serialization of these acts of various worships. They can and should be performed in concert. There are some interdependencies between the various worships. An example is provided in the context of "Taqwa" as discussed in Theorem 1 on page 129. As long as the interfaces and the feedback loops between the worships in the three dimensions are respected, the acts of worship can occur in any sequence and combinations. In fact, the real value is in correctly integrating the worships in the three dimensions so that life becomes a harmonious melody.

The focus of this chapter is to explore the spiritual worships from the perspective of an individual. The discussion from the perspective of the Ummah will be presented in chapter 6.

5.1 Purpose of spiritual worship

Muslims know that there is a greater design of Allah in the creation, as Quran 44:38-40 says:

"We created not the heavens, the earth, and all between them, merely in (idle) sport:

We created them not except for just ends: but most of them do not understand.

Verily the Day of Sorting Out is the time appointed for all of them".

This purpose goes well beyond the conquest of the physical universe or peace on Earth, that were discussed in chapters 3 and 4.

The final abode of the mankind is with Allah: Quran 10:4: "To Him will be your return of all of you. The promise of Allah is true and sure. It is He Who beginneth the process of Creation and repeateth it …"; Quran 36:83: "So glory to Him in Whose hands is the dominion of all things; and to Him will ye be all brought back"; and Quran 84:6: "O thou man! verily thou art ever toiling on towards the Lord painfully toiling but thou shalt meet Him".

Muslims live their lives knowing that they want to meet their Lord, as in Quran 2:46: "Who bear in mind the certainty that they are to meet their Lord and that they are to return to Him". The meeting with Allah is the purpose supreme. It is not a means to another goal.

If it were possible to achieve the final goal of meeting Allah in the spiritual dimension without the efforts in the physical and ethical dimensions, then it would be a waste to spend that effort. In that case Quran would not have prescribed any worships that were not needed. On the contrary, as we discussed in chapters 3 and 4, Allah has given us explicit prescription to perform worship in the physical and ethical dimensions. Those are therefore necessary worships for the purpose of meeting with Allah. And it is easy to understand why.

The spirituality is based on Taqwa, which depends on a profound understanding (developed via worship in physical dimension), and a sincere commitment to that understanding (developed via worship in ethical dimension). "Taqwa" is discussed in Theorem 1 on page 129. Taqwa is a prerequisite for mankind to embark on the spiritual journey, a journey that culminates in meeting with Allah. Indeed, Taqwa is a prerequisite to derive guidance from Quran, as in Quran 2:2: "This is the Book; in it is guidance sure without doubt to those who fear Allah (Muttaqeen)".

The example of the Prophet (S) is very instructive in this regard. He made great observations of his environment. He demonstrated his profound understanding of his environment via his accomplishments in the affairs of the society as well as mundane activities like trading in commodities. He displayed a highly sophisticated Taqwa through his ethical conduct. Only then Allah's mercy granted him spiritual enlightenment. This spiritual enlightenment however was not enough to secure a permanent closeness to Allah. The prophet went considerably farther. He established peace on troubled parts of the Earth where there was no peace before; and he found it necessary to excel in spiritual and secular dimensions in order to accomplish this. Almost as soon as he accomplished this task, he wasted no time to hasten and meet with his Lord.

What is expected of Muslims is no different from what the Prophet clearly exemplified and demonstrated in actions.

5.2 The Five Pillars

Muslims strive to stay true to their nature, in accord with Quran 30:30: "So set thou thy face steadily and truly to the Faith: (Establish) Allah's handiwork according to the pattern on which He has made mankind: no change (let there be) in the work (wrought) by Allah: that is the standard Religion: but most among mankind understand not".

During this spiritual journey, Muslims get help of formal activities that are often referred to as the five pillars. It is clear from the outset that these activities are not objectives in themselves: rather, they are Quranic recommendations to accomplish the journey towards the final goal. Of course, the popular terminology that refers to these activities as "pillars" already contains this implication. The pillars have no independent existence except to support the structure for which they are introduced. Similarly, Quranic recommendations discussed in the following subsections are not the objectives in themselves; they are introduced to aid Muslims, both individually and as a society, to achieve the purpose of the spiritual worships.

The articles of Iman together constitute the first pillar. It is necessary so that the individual can correctly understand her or his journey and recognize the signs along the way. This pillar provides the mindset to enable the other spiritual activities to be properly practiced and to prove useful.

The system of Iman that constitutes the first pillar is rather abstract. Quran recognizes the danger that such an abstract language can pose to the traveler on the spiritual journey, who is used to the physical environment. The Iman system is therefore coupled with formal physical activities such as the prayer, the charity, the fasting, and the pilgrimage. These activities constitute the remaining four pillars. They are not abstract. They are spiritual worships even though they are physical activities. This is because they produce results that can be physically observed and spiritually experienced. As discussed in Theorem 2 on page 139, this is a common characteristic of all spiritual worships. They simultaneously manifest themselves in the physical world as well as the spiritual world.

5.2.1 Pillar: The articles of Iman

In their effort to meet Allah, Muslims undertake a spiritual journey. The progress made by the traveler is measurable in terms of its observable effects in the physical world, in accord with the law of shadows discussed in Theorem 2 on page 139. The signs along this journey are written in a spiritual language. The articles of Iman provide the vocabulary and constructs of this language.

In this sense, these articles of Iman are distinct from the concept of Taqwa, which otherwise forms the foundation of spirituality.

These articles of Iman are described in this section. They are listed in Quran 2:177: "It is not righteousness that ye turn your faces towards East or West; But it is righteousness--- to believe in God and the Last Day, and the Angels, and the Book, and the Messengers; to spend of your substance, out of love for Him, for your kin, for orphans, for the needy, for the wayfarer, for those who ask, and for the ransom of slaves; to be steadfast in prayer, and practice regular charity; to fulfill the contracts which ye have made; and to be firm and patient, in pain (or suffering) and adversity, and throughout all periods of panic. Such are the people of truth, the God-fearing".

Same articles are asserted in Quran 4:136: "O ye who believe! believe in Allah and his Apostle and the scripture which He sent to those before (him). And who denieth Allah His angels His Books His Apostles and the Day of Judgment hath gone far far astray".

Iman in Allah

First and foremost is the Iman in Allah. The word Allah can be thought of as "Al-Ilah". The Iman in Allah means that there is no god other than the only God. This concept includes in itself the concept of oneness that cannot be analyzed into components, as in Quran 112: "Say: He is Allah the One and Only; Allah the Eternal Absolute; He begetteth not nor is He begotten; And there is none like unto Him".

The benefits of Iman in Allah are so tremendous that they require a treatise by themselves. However, I would mention few that I personally find too compelling. The foremost among these is the freedom that the Muslim individual enjoys in every walk of life. An important corollary is the tremendous strength that the Muslim individual enjoys because of this freedom. This freedom and strength is very observable among Muslims, not only in spiritual dimension but also in all physical and ethical aspects as well.

This might seem paradoxical to the uninitiated. The word Muslim literally means submission. Muslims are servants of Allah. How then can they be "free" and "strong"? However, this is the slavery that liberates freedom; this is the submission that defines strength.

If Iman in Allah does not produce free and strong individuals, then the individual in question must take a step back and re-examine the situation.

Iman in Quran

Muslims hold it as evident that Quran is Allah's guidance to mankind, as in Quran 15:9: "We have without doubt sent down the Message; and We will assuredly guard it (from corruption)".

Quran is a book of guidance, and not a book of commandments. Quran treats its followers with respect and does not issue inflexible commandments. As explained in section 4.3, Quran bases its guidance on understanding and commitment to that understanding (Taqwa).

Quran was revealed in stages, many a time in the very limited scope of a concrete practical situation. This created a necessary binding between Quranic Ayahs and the concrete situations that were addressed through them. This binding is the necessary consequence of the dependence of the guidance on the space-time dimension with respect to the practical situation addressed by an Ayah, the society within which the situation occurred, and the historical time of the occurrence. Today Muslims posit that Quranic Ayahs are of more general validity than what the limited environment of their revelation would warrant; and they also do so with a degree of inflexibility. Yes, it is true. However, it is a very difficult task to generalize these Ayahs through a process that de-couples them from their space-time environment. A sophisticated framework is needed to accomplish this generalization. Such a framework does not currently exist.

The need for this framework was recognized right at the outset by none other than Mohammad (S) himself. Thus, the Prophet (S) commanded his companions to compile Quran using a sequence that is very different from the sequence in which it was revealed. Compiled in this fashion, Quran has 114 chapters that often combine verses that were revealed at very different times and occasions. There are however two important points to digest.

1. Mohammad was indeed the most capable person to understand Quran. However, the practical manifestation of this understanding was much more limited compared to the extent to which he understood it. This is a necessary consequence of the intrinsic limitation of the human experience due to the space-time dimension. The space-time of Mohammad allowed only a limited manifestation of his understanding of Quran in the practical situations that were encountered, the way they were encountered, the people involved and their level of understanding, and the set of available means.

2. Many Quranic Ayahs nicely mapped on to the concrete situations on the ground. Their meanings and significance were many a time quite obvious within that context. Hence there was less need to generalize these Ayahs, and virtually no need for the framework to facilitate such generalization.

Hence the Prophet's example does not often enlighten Muslims about the subtleties of generalization and the guidelines towards a framework for the same.

There are very real difficulties in developing a framework to generalize those Ayahs of Quran that mapped very closely to concrete realities on the ground. The first step is to sincerely recognize these concrete realities, analyze them, and document them. Lot of research is needed for this framework of systematic rules and procedures for the task at hand. The task is made next to impossible because the concrete situation that the Ayahs addressed are now not known, except for a handful of cases.

Challenging though it is, such a framework for generalization is very much needed to eliminate, or at least to substantially reduce, the ad hoc opinion-based approach that has been used so far, which has given rise to sectarianism among Muslims. The consequences of sectarianism have dwarfed the giant-like posture of Muslims. They have placed Quran in a light that is subject to widespread misunderstanding as well as outright mischief in some cases.

Iman in Mohammad (S)

Muslims hold it as evident that Mohammad as the "rasool" of Allah. Quran as the divine guidance was revealed to mankind through the medium of Mohammad (S), Quran 26 :192-196:

"Verily this is a Revelation from the Lord of the Worlds:

With it came down the Spirit of Faith and Truth (Ruhul Amin)

To thy heart and mind that thou mayest admonish

In the perspicuous Arabic tongue.

Without doubt it is (announced) in the mystic Books of former peoples."

It means that the Angel of Allah under an explicit command from Allah brought appropriate portions of Quran to Mohammad (S) and he was assigned the task by Allah to propagate Quran to all folks. See Quran 19:64: "(The angels say:) "We descend not but by command of thy Lord: …"

The Prophet received Quranic revelation directly from Allah via the medium of Gabriel. The person of Mohammad is beyond any suspicion that he may have manipulated the guidance in any way. Even if he wanted to manipulate Quran, one might recall that Allah was the real master of the situation and Mohammad was merely serving as an instrument of Allah, as indeed was the case with Gabriel who also was serving as an instrument of Allah. Indeed, Allah chooses whatever means He decides to use in a particular situation.

Muslims also regard Mohammad (S) as a perfect example of how one should use Quran to live one's life, see Quran 68:4: "And thou (standest) on an exalted standard of character". The example of the Prophet(S) is referred to as the Sunnah of the Prophet. Muslims have developed an elaborate science to collect, authenticate, report, and interpret events from the life of the Prophet. These are recorded in the books of Hadith with great fidelity.

While the authenticity and absolute correctness of Quran is established beyond any doubt, the same is not true for the recorded Sunnah. At a higher level, even the definition as to what are the sources of Sunnah is controversial. Thus, Sunnis and Shias do not generally use the same sources. There are subdivisions even among Shias and Sunnis. For instance, the Sunnis generally like to adhere to the four Imams. There are, however, differences among the four Imams that are regarded by their followers to be very significant. This has often been a source of grave sectarian consequences.

There is of course a very urgent need to build a bridge over such divisions. Their consequences have proved to be very damaging and a source of spiritual and secular retardation. Despite all the confusion about the sources of Sunnah and the very many sects subscribing to different opinions, there has been very little research (versus opinions) to analyze the question as to what Sunnah is!

Is Sunnah the description in the books of Hadith? The answer has to be a no. This is because the Hadith descriptions are addressing isolated incidents, events, and occasions. On the other hand, the Sunnah of the Prophet is the entire life he lived. His life was the continuously flowing events and activities, which he partook or performed. These were superbly inter-connected into a dynamic scheme of things that was most ingenious and insightful. The Prophet did not merely follow the rituals; rather he specified them with a most clearly defined focus. The books of Hadith include none of the ingenuity, insight, and focus. As a result, those who insist that Sunnah equates with the collection in the six books of Hadith have made Sunnah into a inflexibly mechanical process without its most essential parts like the insight and the focus.

The narration in the Hadith approaches nowhere close to the splendor that was the life of Mohammad (S). They merely describe in words what happened in living colors: and then they describe only a small discrete set of events out of an infinity of events in the continuum that was the life of the Prophet (S). Hadith have none of the superb inter connectivity, none of the insightful dynamism, and none of the liveliness that was part of the Sunnah. Even if the descriptions of the Hadith are taken to be correct, they still miss all the above-mentioned aspects that are indeed an essential part of the Sunnah.

But there is more! The context of the Hadith is also often missing. This context includes important information. Was the setting an informal close-knit gathering or a stage meant for a serious address to Muslims? What were the intentions behind the statements that the Prophet made, or the actions that he performed? Was he making a casual suggestion to an individual? Did he mean the words to apply to all that were present? Did he want to address all Muslims that existed at that time? Did he intend to include the posterity of Muslims to come when he made his statement or performed his action? All these are valid inquiries and the books of Hadith are not very descriptive in that regard. These are some of the shortcomings of the books of Hadith in representing the Sunnah of the Prophet (S).

Iman in Judgment

Quran is very explicit that humans will be accountable for their thoughts, plans, intentions, and actions, as discussed in previous chapter. Quran clearly states that all people will be brought back to Allah. Muslims firmly know of this accountability and of eventual return to Allah.

The details of the judgment with respect to the timing and execution are with Allah alone. Such details are not needed for the spiritual journey that Muslims undertake.

The Iman in Angels

Quran refers to the Iman in Angels together with the Iman in Allah, the Books, the Prophets, and the Judgment, see Quran 2:285: "The Apostle believeth in what hath been revealed to him from his Lord as do the men of faith. Each one (of them) believeth in Allah His angels His books and His Apostles ..."

Further it is warned that not to have such Iman is equivalent to serious misguidance, see Quran 4:136: "O ye who believe! believe in Allah and his Apostle and the scripture which He sent to those before (him). And who denieth Allah His angels His Books His Apostles and the Day of Judgment hath gone far far astray".

Muslims have Iman in the Angels, as directed by Quran.

However, it is not clear what the nature of Angels is or what the significance of this Iman in Angels is. Quran has used the concept of Angels that was very familiar to the people of Arabia. However, the concept as known to the people of Arabia was ridden with grave misunderstandings. Quran felt it necessary to make certain crucial corrections. For instance, they used to think that the Angels are female, see Quran 43:19 "And they make into females angels who themselves serve Allah. Did they witness their creation? Their evidence will be recorded and they will be called to account"! Some used to think that they are the daughters of Allah, and some used to hold grudge against certain angels. All these attitudes are categorically condemned.

Quran declares that the Angels are but Servants of Allah and creation of Allah.

The question arises, why Quran insists that one creation of Allah must profess Iman in another creation of Allah?

As far as I understand, there is profound significance in this. Whenever we are asked to have Iman in a creation it implies the exist-

81

ence of that creation and the validity of a role or a function that it fulfils regarding mankind under Allah's commandment. For example, we have Iman in the Prophets to recognize the institute of Prophet-hood, its function and its relation to our life. We have Iman in the Judgment for similar reasons: we agree to the concept of accountability for our actions and we recognize that we must conclude our spiritual journey with a final return to Allah. We have Iman in the books to recognize that they are indeed valid guidance from Allah and to use this guidance to better our lives to prepare ourselves for the final abode.

Why do we confess Iman in Angels? It must be to recognize a particular function and role that the Angels perform regarding mankind, of course under the commands of Allah. What is this role? Quran has the answer, see Quran 35:1: "Praise be to Allah Who created (out of nothing) the heavens and the earth Who made the angels messengers with wings two or three or four (Pairs): He adds to Creation as He pleases: for Allah has power over all things". It appears that the Angels communicate messages under the command of Allah. Allah created Angels for this purpose because He adds to Creation as He pleases: for Allah has power over all things.

Now what is special about this role to perform the communication of messages? It must be something that impacts humans and the humans themselves are not capable of such communications. For if it does not impact the humans, then Quran would not require Iman in it. Likewise, if the humans can perform this function, then there is no compelling need to have Iman in the role of the Angels to duplicate the capability.

It therefore follows that the role of the Angels must not be possible to be performed by the humans, and it must not be subject to "conquest" by mankind like the physical dimension is. The special functions that are symbolized by the creation of Angels must therefore be outside of the physical dimension. We shall use the term "spiritual dimension" (in contrast to the physical dimension) to denote the space in which this operation by the Angels takes place.

The Iman in Angels therefore recognizes the existence of a spiritual dimension and the special communication that take place in the spiritual dimension. These communications bring the special "amr" of Allah for the mankind as well as for other creation, see Quran 97:4: "Therein come down the angels and the Spirit by Allah's permission on every errand". This special "amr" originates from the "spiritual dimension" which is outside of the "physical dimension".

When the Angels bring the special "amr" of Allah into the physical dimension, the world is impacted by this special "amr".

Let us comment on "... with wings two or three or four ..." in Quran 35:1. Abdullah Yusuf Ali inserted "(pairs")" in his translation. That is inspired by our experience with birds! But are Angles like birds? We have no experience with birds with one wing, so we imagine the wings to occur in pairs! But does Quran mean literal wings like the wings of a bird? That we do not know. However, there can be a scientific notion in this Quranic statement. We know that the limit of the speed of communication in the physical dimension is the speed of light, and let us denote by the letter c the numeric value of the speed of light. According to the theory of special relativity, there can be no speed of communication faster than c. Is Quran stating that communication speeds faster than c are possible for Angels? These speeds are described as 2c, 3c, and 4c. If this be so, one could begin to imagine the scales that apply in the spiritual dimension.

While the existence of Angels by no means diminishes the importance of the scientific research, it does bring home the fact that the accomplishments of science take place in a physical dimension that does not include those spiritual functions that are attributed to the Angels.

The Iman in Angels therefore means that there will always be special impacts on human life that the humans cannot control or manipulate through scientific research. This is a limitation of the processes of the scientific research because it confines itself to the physical dimension. It is not a human limitation; rather, it is the limitation of a human activity. Humans are created as spiritual beings and they can always communicate with Allah; they just cannot communicate with Allah using the currently limited means of the scientific methods.

Further, such a function cannot be deduced within the science itself in a self-consistent manner, and it can only be introduced into science through external means, such as by hand.

However, this takes place without violating the laws of the physical universe discussed in section 3.4 because these represent the Amr of Allah that He ordained as part of the act of creation. The special "amr" of Allah is subject to the overarching Amr of Allah. For example, the law of causality is respected, and the law of gravity is not violated. It would, however, appear that the special "amr" of Allah that arrives from the spiritual dimension is richer than the language of the laws in the physical universe is capable of expression. Therefore, a translation must be performed from the special "amr" of Allah into the laws of the physical universe, and this translation must be one way, and it must be one to many. The one-way nature of the translation means that the special "amr" of Allah cannot be deduced by observing the physical phenomena taking place under the physical laws. One to many aspect of the translation means that one special "amr" of Allah can be translated into the physical laws in many possible ways; but once the translation is done the effect on the physical dimension collapses into one result. The mechanism that enables this to occur are not understood; though it would appear that it is embedded into the special role of the Angels.

The Imsn in Angels brings home a foundational principle in Islam: namely that Allah is not a passive God like a "prime mover" in Greek philosophy; rather, Allah is an "Active God" who actively manages the affairs under clearly established principles and rules.

5.2.2 Pillar: The Salat

Salat means a connection and connectivity. In Arabic language AT&T Inc is known as شركة الاتصالات; the word Salat here has the same root as in the word Salat in prayer. It means communication or connectivity. Salat is an instrument to get connected with Allah. The Prophet stated the concept by declaring that Salat is a Meraj for the people with Iman.

It addresses the connection and connectivity between the people and Allah. It could be visualized as a physical meeting between the two together with the protocols for such a meeting. The meeting, among other things, is intended to be a two-way communicative exchange.

Salat is also connectivity between people. That is easier to see, as people gather and connect during the Jama'at for the Salat.

*

The prescription of Salat as an instrument of spiritual emancipation is nothing unique to the followers of Islam. It has been a constant theme for all nations:

Quran 14:37: "O our Lord! I have made some of my offspring to dwell in a valley without cultivation by thy Sacred House; in order O our Lord that they may establish regular prayer: so fill the hearts of some among men with love towards them and feed them with Fruits: so that they may give thanks"; Quran 20:14 "Verily I am Allah: there is no god but I: so serve thou me (only) and establish regular prayer for celebrating My praise"; and Quran 21:73: "And We made them leaders guiding (men) by Our Command and We sent them inspiration to do good deeds to establish regular prayers and to practice regular charity; and they constantly served Us (and Us only)".

Quran invites us for the Salat with one theme that is common throughout. Quran prescribes that we "establish" the Salat, not just go through it as a ritual. This establishment is not recommended as a mere ritual but as a meaningful institution in our society as well as in our individual lives. It is to be established with Taqwa and with the full gravity of realization of its role in our lives, as a meeting with Allah.

Failing this, Quran provides a counter example, Quran 19:59: "But after them there followed a posterity who missed prayers and followed after lusts: soon then will they face Destruction". Indeed, people who failed to establish Salat as an institution, versus just doing it as a ritual, wasted their prayers and led themselves into following their lustful inclinations, which in turn took them on the path to destruction.

*

As stated earlier, the Salat is an instrument for spiritual emancipation. As an instrument, it is not an objective in itself. What then is the purpose of Salat?

Please recall from our earlier discussion that the final abode of mankind is with Allah. Further, all worship is intended for the benefit of the worshipper alone, and Allah does not benefit from it. The Salat is therefore entirely for the benefit of the worshipper. Quran prescribes certain objectives for the Salat. If the worshipper offers a Salat that meets these objectives, then the purpose of Salat is fulfilled. On the other hand, if the Salat is practiced merely as a ritual but Quranic objectives for the Salat are not achieved, then this ritualistic practice does not qualify as Salat, and it is the same whether the ritual is observed or not.

Quran mentions some expected benefits of the Salat that are physically observable. A person offering the Salat should use them as a checklist for the purpose of measuring the efficacy of his or her efforts. Some examples are given below.

o   Salat should be used as a source of help, as in Quran 2:153: "O ye who believe! seek help with patient perseverance and prayer:

87

for Allah is with those who patiently persevere". Please note that this verse recommends the virtues of the "Sabr" and "Salat" in order to receive help. The individual role of the two virtues as well as their inter relationships are, however, not elaborated.

o   Salat should keep us away from some bad traits, for example, acts that are shameful and unjust, as in Quran 29:45: "Recite what is sent of the Book by inspiration to thee and establish Regular Prayer: for Prayer restrains from shameful and unjust deeds; …".

*

While proclaiming righteousness to others, we must not forget to examine our own selves, Quran 2:44: "Do ye enjoin right conduct on the people and forget (to practice it) yourselves and yet ye study the Scripture? Will ye not understand?" We must analyze our activities, even when we do them in apparent commitment to righteousness; in particular, we must examine if our establishment of Salat meets Quranic objectives. Are the Muslims becoming strong with the help of Salat? Are Muslims clean of the shameful and unjust acts? Unfortunately, there are abundant indications that the currently established practice of Salat falls visibly short of meeting the objectives that Quran specifies for the Salat. The "establishment of Salat" has been stripped of its grandeur and it has been gradually reduced to a mere ritual. This must change.

Muslims have developed a simplistic notion that Allah will ask them if they offered the canonical Salat, and they can answer it in the affirmative even if they have gone through the Salat merely in a ritualistic sense, without meeting its objectives. This is unfortunate. There is no human activity that is recognized as having been completed without reference to what it accomplished with respect to its objectives. Allah has clearly described the objectives of the Salat, and no individual shall be able to answer the call in affirmative unless those objectives have been accomplished.

5.2.3 Pillar: The Zakat

Wealth of a person is defined as what Allah has bestowed upon that person. Quran discusses the sharing of wealth in that context, as in Quran 8-3: "Who establish regular prayers and spend (freely) out of the gifts We have given them for sustenance:"

Everything belongs to Allah. He gives wealth to whomever He wills, as in Quran 42-19: "Gracious is Allah to His servants: He gives Sustenance to whom He pleases: and He has Power and can carry out His Will." The sharing of wealth with other human beings is at two levels. One level is made obligatory for all with respect to what they possess beyond their needs; the second level is to voluntarily spend out of love for Allah, see Quran 2:177: "... ; to spend of your substance out of love for Him for your kin for orphans for the needy for the wayfarer for those who ask and for the ransom of slaves; ..."

*

It may be recalled that Iman is a necessary precondition for all spiritual worships. This is true also for the charity. Without Iman, no sharing of wealth is admissible, as in Quran 9:54: "The only reasons why their contributions are not accepted are: that they reject Allah and His apostle; that they come to prayer without earnestness; and that they offer contributions unwillingly."

Muslims are encouraged to spend what they can spare and spend it on near and dear one's as well as on strangers; see Quran 2:219: ... They ask thee how much they are to spend; say: "What is beyond your needs." Thus doth Allah make clear to you His Signs: in order that ye may consider"; and Quran 2:215: "They ask thee what they should spend (in charity). Say: Whatever ye spend that is good is for parents and kindred and orphans and those in want and for wayfarers. And whatever ye do that is good Allah knoweth it well."

*

The sharing of wealth is not a new worship among Muslims. It was also prescribed to other nations; see Quran 5:12: "Allah did aforetime take a Covenant from the Children of Israel and We appointed twelve captains among them and Allah said: "I am with you: if ye (but) establish regular prayers *practice regular charity* believe in My apostles honor and assist them and *loan to Allah a beautiful loan* verily I will wipe out from you your evils and admit you to gardens with rivers flowing beneath; but if any of you after this resisteth faith he hath truly wandered from the path of rectitude"; and Quran 21:73: "And We made them leaders guiding (men) by Our Command and We sent them inspiration to do good deeds to establish regular prayers and to *practice regular charity*; and they constantly served Us (and Us only)".

The purpose of this spiritual worship is to achieve economic parity among Muslims and also to meet the needs of the society that it may face from time to time. The spending of the wealth that Allah gives us is a worship that brings us closer to Allah who appreciates our efforts. These aspects are described in Quran 2:262: "Those who spend their substance in the cause of Allah and follow not up their gifts with reminders of their generosity or with injury for them their reward is with their Lord; on them shall be no fear nor shall they grieve"; Quran 9:91: "There is no blame on those who are infirm or ill or who find no resources to spend (on the cause) if they are sincere (in duty) to Allah and His apostle: no ground (of complaint) can there be against such as do right: and Allah is Oft-Forgiving Most Merciful"; Quran 2:274: "Those who (in charity) spend of their goods by night and by day in secret and in public have their reward with their Lord: on them shall be no fear nor shall they grieve"; and Quran 2:261: "The parable of those who spend their substance in the way of Allah is that of a grain of corn: it groweth seven ears and each ear hath a hundred grains. Allah giveth manifold increase to whom He pleaseth; and Allah careth for all and He knoweth all things".

It may be observed that Quran often talks about the Salat and the Zakat together in the same sentence. There are only very few instances, where Quran talks about Salat without also talking about the Zakat and vice versa. One such instance is an interesting invitation for the reader to meditate on: here Quran emphasizes that the compassion of Allah is Omni present, the punishment of Allah will be selectively applied to whoever is to meet it, and the fact that those who spend to please Allah shall see His compassion. See for one of the rare occasion where charity is discussed without explicitly accompanying it with Salat, Quran 7:156: ""And ordain for us that which is good in this life

91

and in the hereafter: for we have turned unto Thee." He said: "with My punishment I visit whom I will; but My mercy extendeth to all things. That (Mercy) I shall ordain for those who do right and *practice regular charity* and those who believe in Our signs"".

The coupling between the Salat and the Zakat is not without significance. Salat is individual's relationship with Allah; the sharing of wealth is the individual's relationship with humanity. They go hand in hand: one being a reflection of the other. Thus, a practical measure of one's sincerity towards Allah is one's compassion for the humans.

This intrinsic relationship between one's attitude towards Allah and the same towards the humans is a constant and persistent theme in Quran. This is one example of the "Law of shadows" that we will discuss later in Theorem 2 on page 139.

*

When we spend our wealth as a worship, we must constantly examine how well we are fulfilling the purpose of this worship. We must always seek better and more optimal ways to spend our wealth such that the underlying objectives are accomplished with ever increasing proficiency.

Muslims have done reasonably well at feeling compassion for those amongst them who are less fortunate. They have consistently shared their wealth with those without it. However, they often view it as an obligation rather than an opportunity.

The impact of this sharing has been largely at a local scale. The local effects can nevertheless add-up to produce an impact at a more extended scale. For instance, over the past few decades, Muslims of

USA have shared their wealth and developed Mosques. This has dotted USA with Mosques and afforded the Muslim community a very valuable infrastructure. It is now being used to support additional objectives like schools, seminars, and voter registration. These achievements are not small. They have produced a momentum that can lead to rapid development in future.

These developments can be accelerated if Muslims engineer their efforts for results at the extended scales, versus letting these effects slowly evolve under the prevailing dynamics of the space-time. Through their focused efforts, Muslims can achieve even greater success by enlarging their perspective. They can view the Islamic institution of "sharing wealth" as a tremendous opportunity to be systematically used at a more global scale. Muslims can successfully pool these resources for addressing the national and international needs. There are about two billion Muslims in the World today. Every year they spend their wealth on Zakat, Fitrah, and charity in general, as well as on Qurbani. Collectively this does add up to a significant amount every year. Fitrah, Zakat, Sadaqat, and Qurbani would add up to tens of billions of dollars each year.

If it is systematically collected and accumulated over few years, it will add up to a serious economic forum comparable in import to the forums like the World Bank and the International Monetary Fund (IMF). What is even more significant is the fact that the Islamic mechanisms guarantee the replenishment of this fund at the grass root level. No such guarantees exist for the World Bank and the IMF whose survival depends on the interests and willingness of the donor countries. Existing forums like the Islamic development Bank and the Organization of Islamic Conference can play a role towards making these resources demonstrate their international potential.

5.2.4 Pillar: The Saum

The term "Saum" means to abstain. It refers to the practice of fasting during the month of Ramadan, Quran 2-185: "Ramadan is the (month) in which was sent down the Qur'an as a guide to mankind also clear (Signs) for guidance and judgment (between right and wrong). So everyone of you who is present (at his home) during that month should spend it in fasting but if anyone is ill or on a journey the prescribed period (should be made up) by days later. Allah intends every facility for you He does not want to put you to difficulties. (He wants you) to complete the prescribed period and to glorify Him in that He has guided you; and perchance ye shall be grateful".

*

The practice of fasting is not new, Quran 2:183: "O you who have attained to faith! Fasting is ordained for you as it was ordained for those before you, so that you might remain conscious of God" (M. Asad). The whole Lunar month of Ramadan is for fasting. However, if one is sick or is traveling, then one may miss the fasting for the corresponding days of Ramadan and make up the count after the month of Ramadan.

In certain circumstances, it may be impractical to fast. In that case an alternate act of piety may be performed in lieu of fasting. This alternate act is feeding the poor, Quran 2:184: "(Fasting) for a fixed number of days; but if any of you is ill or on a journey the prescribed number (should be made up) from days later. For those who can do it (with hardship) is a ransom the feeding of one that is indigent. But he that will give more of his own free will it is better for him and it is better for you that ye fast if ye only knew". The fasting itself can be used as an act of piety to compensate for some sins. Such acts that are acceptable as compensation for the sins include to free a slave, to feed and clothe the poor, and to fast, Quran 5:89: "Allah will not call you to account for what is futile in your oaths but He will call you to account for your deliberate oaths: for expiation feed then indigent persons on a scale of the average for the food of your families; or clothe them; or give a slave his freedom. If that is beyond your means fast for three days. That is the expiation for the oaths ye have sworn. But keep to your oaths. Thus doth Allah make clear to you His Signs that ye may be grateful".

It is worthwhile to take a pause and note how Quran freely interchanges Allah's worship with acts that are for the benefit of mankind. Thus, an inability to fast or an explicit sin of not keeping a vow may be compensated by feeding and clothing the poor or to set a slave free. This concept of equivalence between the worship of Allah and doing good deeds for the benefit of mankind is a distinguished feature of Quran. This is an example of the "Law of shadows" described in Theorem 2 on page 139. It is indeed a constant and persistent theme in Quran. It allows the worshipper's spiritual emancipation to be physically visible through his or her compassion for the mankind. A spiritual emancipation that does not manifest itself in a proportional compassion and love for the mankind is of doubtful validity.

*

As the name implies, one purpose of Saum is to provide training at abstinence. The abstinence from food and drink as well as from sex and eroticism is only a minimal thing. The Saum also implies more abstract cases of abstinence. These include abstaining from ego trips, abstaining from temptation to be less than generous and compassionate in one's dealings with people, and abstaining from time spent in pursuits that are less than devotional to Allah. As is the case with other spiritual worships, the ultimate purpose of fasting is to make the individual constantly conscious of Allah, i.e., Muttaqi, and that is for the good of the worshipper's own self.

*

Muslims do reasonably well at this worship. They fast, study Quran, do additional Salat, and practice acts of charity and kindness. These accomplishments are visible among Muslims in their superior disposition with respect to selfless acts of "giving" without any expectation for reciprocation. They are good at displaying acts of beauty that might seem 'senseless' to one who is used to a give and take, and not used to just giving only.

However, there is clearly room for improvement. Muslims devote much effort for Quranic recitation, though the emphasis is usually to complete the recitation of the whole Quran, without a proportional effort to understand and research the meanings of its message and guidance. There is also room for Muslims to organize group activities focused at doing good deeds for the society and for resolving practical situations facing the members of the community at any particular place and time.

5.2.5 Pillar: The Haj

Haj requirement is proclaimed to the people to come to the Kaaba despite all the difficulties with respect to the finance and travel and other logistics, if they can overcome such difficulties. There is a detailed description in Quran 22:27-31:

"And proclaim the Pilgrimage among men: they will come to thee on foot and (mounted) on every kind of camel lean on account of journeys through deep and distant mountain highways;

"That they may witness the benefits (provided) for them and celebrate the name of Allah through the Days appointed over the cattle which He has provided for them (for sacrifice): then eat ye thereof and feed the distressed ones in want."

"Then let them complete the rites prescribed for them perform their vows and (again) circumambulate the Ancient House."

"Such (is the Pilgrimage): whoever honors the sacred rites of Allah for him it is good in the sight of his Lord. Lawful to you (for food in pilgrimage) are cattle except those mentioned to you (as exceptions): but shun the abomination of idols and shun the word that is false.

Being true in faith to Allah and never assigning partners to Him: if anyone assigns partners to Allah he is as if he had fallen from heaven and been snatched up by birds or the wind had swooped (like a bird on its prey) and thrown him into a far-distant place".

*

Islam did not introduce Hajj. The Arab community prior to Islam practiced it. Islam endorsed this practice with a very explicit focus and purpose, while abandoning some meaningless ingredients of it that had become the custom. For instance, they used to not enter their houses through the front door during the Haj, and would use the back doors; Quran corrected this practice: Quran 2:189: "They ask thee concerning the new moons. Say: they are but signs to mark fixed periods of time in (the affairs of) men and for pilgrimage. It is no virtue if ye enter your houses from the back; it is virtue if ye fear Allah. Enter houses through the proper doors and fear Allah that ye may prosper."

Logistics concerning the journey for Hajj are recognized, and it is an obligation only for those who can afford such logistics, Quran 3:97: "In it are signs manifest; (for example) the Station of Abraham; whoever enters it attains security; pilgrimage thereto is a duty men owe to Allah those who can afford the journey; but if any deny faith Allah stands not in need of any of his creatures".

*

The Hajj has a many-fold purpose; Quran 22:28 describes three specific purposes. First, there is the more visible purpose that affords physical benefits to the Pilgrims. Second, there is the spiritual purpose to seek closeness to Allah. Third, there is a social benefit, for example through feeding the distressed in society. Quran 22:31 also mentions the purpose to develop one's Iman and realize the glory of Tauheed.

As is generally true, if the purpose is not met, the observance of the mere rituals is of no avail. Quran 22:31 tells us that failure in the objective is like a fall from grace and being completely lost.

If the purpose of the worship is kept in focus, the ritualistic part is flexible. Thus, one may seek business opportunities during the Hajj and do works of recognized benefit to oneself and the community. Quran 2:198: "It is no crime in you if ye seek of the bounty of your Lord (during Pilgrimage). Then when ye pour down from (Mount) Arafat celebrate the praises of Allah at the Sacred Monument and celebrate His praises as He has directed you even though before this ye went astray."

*

The Hajj is a great opportunity for Muslims to conduct the affairs of the Ummah. The Ummah now consists of vast geographical regions with diverse human and natural resources. The leaderships of these regions can put the practice of Hajj to good advantage for the Ummah. However, no such thing is currently done. This is a colossal failure to act in the interest of the Ummah.

At the individual level, the Hajj is a worship like other spiritual worships. It is not clear from Quranic prescriptions if Hajj is unique with respect to its spiritual benefits, as compared to the spiritual benefits from other forms of spiritual worship.

Though not explicitly mentioned, travel by itself is a benefit to the pilgrim. This includes observing the signs of Allah in new places, meeting other pilgrims, and experiencing a global vibe. This enriches pilgrim's world-view; it is like turning a page in the book of life.

5.2.6 Mechanisms of Spiritual worships

The spiritual worships are performed in the form of physical activities. Every such activity gets a response from Allah, see Quran 2:186: "And if My servants ask thee about me – behold, I am near; I respond to the call of him who calls, whenever he calls unto Me, …" (M. Asad). Islam prescribes four specific forms of physical activities that constitute formalized spiritual worships. They also are referred to as the four pillars, and we will discuss them in this section.

It is understood that Allah responds to each such worship activity when a person performs it. Therefore, these activities are enablers for an individual to have a genuine two-way communication with Allah. The effects of these activities are for the spiritual emancipation of the individual. However, they are reflected in a solid ethical excellence and physical strength; and this leads to a strong Ummah.

In a spiritual sense, these pillars are not the objectives in themselves. They are the tools for spiritual emancipation through enhancements in Taqwa. Spiritual emancipation manifests itself in ethical excellence, physical strength, and an Ummah that is strong among the nations of the world. In the absence of these manifestations, it is the case that the perceived spiritual emancipation is not real.

The pillars are also tools for further research in the spiritual dimension, for example to understand the laws that operate in the spiritual universe, and to navigate the phenomena in the spiritual universe using those laws. Let us now discuss the mechanism to do research in the spiritual dimension.

There is a special link between the humans and Allah that is symbolized by the Iman in Angels. Further, there is special "amr" from Allah, which can be invoked through the spiritual worships, and the Angels communicate this special "amr".

Worships in the spiritual dimension are specifically intended to enable the humans to communicate with Allah. The response from Allah may come via any means that Allah wills, including the formally recognized mechanism of Allah sending His special "amr" via the Angels.

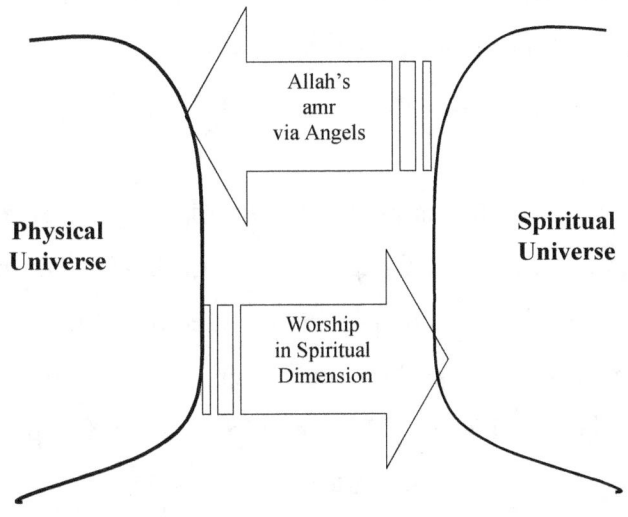

Figure 5-1: Worship in the spiritual dimension enables communication between the physical and spiritual dimensions, carried out via the Angels.

Figure 5-1 illustrates this interface between the spiritual dimension and the physical dimension, which is negotiated via the Angels. The physical and spiritual universes, as well as the Angels, are part of Allah's creation. No statement is made as to where and how they exist:

the only statement is that no communication is possible between these two universes using the techniques derived purely from the research in the physical universe. Such communication can be accomplishable only via the "technology" available in the spiritual dimension.

Allah created mankind with intrinsic capabilities in the spiritual dimension, see Quran 15:29 and 38:72: "When I have fashioned him (in due proportion) and breathed into him of My spirit fall ye down in obeisance unto him"; and Quran 32:9: "But He fashioned him in due proportion and breathed into him something of His spirit. And He gave you (the faculties of) hearing and sight and feeling (and understanding): little thanks do ye give!".

These capabilities in the spiritual dimension allow the humans to reach out to Allah.

This spirituality is as much part of the human beings as are the sensory and intellectual capabilities. This has important consequences: for example, humans do not feel satisfied by achievements in the physical universe alone; and indeed, generally, they also seek to accomplish spiritual emancipation. The worships that Quran specifies in the spiritual dimension are intended for the spiritual emancipation. They enable the humans to communicate with Allah using the laws that govern the spiritual universe. These laws involve the Angels in the mechanism that operates them.

The instruments of research that enable the conquest of the physical universe provide the humans no understanding of the mechanisms through which the spiritual worships work. For this, people are obligated to conduct research in the spiritual dimension.

The spiritual worships that Quran prescribes constitute the tools for this research.

It is possible for the above mechanism to operate in such a way that the worshipper receives an observable advantage in the physical dimension. This would be caused by the special "amr" of Allah, as discussed earlier. Whenever this occurs it does so according to certain rules of invocation that Allah has established.

Rule 1

The special Amr of Allah comes in response to the human worship. It therefore follows that the humans must take the initiative to invoke the Amr.

Rule 2

When appropriate conditions exist, the special "amr" that comes in response to the worship can manifest itself in providing the worshipper with advantage in the physical universe; for example, Quran 8:9-11:

"Remember ye implored the assistance of your Lord and He answered you: "I will assist you with a thousand of the angels ranks on ranks."

Allah made it but a message of hope and an assurance to your heart: (in any case) there is no help except from Allah: and Allah is exalted in power wise.

Remember He covered you with a sort of drowsiness to give you calm as from Himself and He caused rain to descend on you from heaven to clean you therewith to remove from you the stain of satan to strengthen your hearts and to plant your feet firmly therewith".

The rule for invoking such assistance is that, the human must first do everything within their scope to achieve the results, as in Quran 8:60: "Against them make ready your strength to the utmost of your power including steeds of war to strike terror into (the hearts of) the enemies of Allah and your enemies and others besides whom ye may not know but whom Allah doth know. Whatever ye shall spend in the cause of Allah shall be repaid unto you and ye shall not be treated unjustly".

The purpose of the spiritual worships is spiritual emancipation. It is not primarily intended to gain advantage in the physical dimension, though spiritual emancipation by itself brings such advantage. That is a reason that the Prophet invoked this special "amr" from Allah only once in his lifetime, namely at the occasion of Badr which is discussed in Quran.

Therefore, mankind must do everything within their powers to achieve the physical results, Quran 53:39-40: "That man can have nothing but what he strives for; That (the fruit of) his striving will soon come in sight". The special "amr" will not intervene on behalf of Muslims or the non-Muslims, if they fail to properly strive.

It should be noted that all that happens in the creation of Allah, does so according to the Amr of Allah which manifests as the representation by the laws of science to the extent that such laws are valid. In the current discussion we are talking about a "special" "amr" of Allah; signifying only that "amr" which comes in response to the prayer of a worshipper. A simple-minded approach should not be taken towards the special "amr" and its physical consequences; for example, we should not assume a discrete nature of worship and the special "amr" nor a simple one to one correspondence between physical happenings and the special "amr". We have differentiated these cases by using Amr with a lower case as "amr", and we have used the word "special" to qualify it.

Rule 3

The special "amr" of Allah manifests in the physical dimension in complete conformity with the laws of nature.

We discussed in chapter 3 that the laws of Allah are the Amr of Allah as established in the universe. We also refer to these as the laws of nature as they are discovered by the scientists. The special "amr" of Allah is by design conformant to the Amr of Allah which is represented by valid scientific laws.

In the context of Iman in Angels, we have talked about a special "amr" of Allah which is communicated by the Angels. This special "amr" does not alter the general Amr of Allah that he established as part of the creation. Therefore, the special "amr" operates under the general Amr of Allah. One could understand the special "amr" of Allah as a specialized guidance from Allah specialized for the situation at hand. The situation in Badr completely exemplifies it.

There is much in the laws of Allah that the laws of nature, as discovered through scientific research, do not embody. The set of the applicable laws is indeed larger than what the scientific research has discovered. To the extent that the laws that the scientists have discovered represent the laws of nature, they are the laws that Allah manifested through His Amr. These laws that the scientists have discovered are deficient in two essential ways. First, the set of laws is incomplete in the sense that there are many laws that the scientists have not yet discovered. Second, the dynamics of these laws are only partially understood; this is so in many ways, for example, the interrelationships between different laws are not properly understood; and the full sensitivity of a law towards its variables is not known in all regions of its applicability: situations that lead to such phenomena as the "butterfly effect".

Even though the achievements of science are indeed very profound, the above-mentioned limitations are also profound. The prevailing attitude among the scientists is that, no matter how far the sciences advance, the above-mentioned deficiencies of the sciences will remain.

One consequence of these deficiencies is that phenomena can occur that are in perfect accord with the laws of nature and yet they appear to us as miracles. As the human knowledge advances so does the understanding of such phenomena.

*

Let us summarize the discussion in this chapter. The articles of Iman together define the environment for the mental attitude with which the remaining four pillars should be constructed. The ritualistic practices are only as effective as the appropriateness of the mental attitude of the individual who observes those rituals.

The five pillars, together, are intended to provide support for the grand scheme of things that Quran has in mind. The precise role of these worships is determined by the architectural details of how this framework is formulated in a particular space-time environment. The five pillars are thus not the objectives in themselves. They are the tools that Quran recommends in order to achieve the objectives with respect to the individual and the Ummah, see Theorem 3 on page 145.

In a practical sense, the usefulness of the observance of these rituals can be evaluated by considering the impact of the practice on the individual worshipper as well as the position of the Ummah among the nations of the world. The value of observing these rituals derives from the extent to which the underlying objectives are met. Without paying attention to these objectives, the rituals are not at all meaningful. Please note that Quran makes it abundantly clear that the worships are for the worshipper only, and Allah does not need them. Further, Quran declares that a person is valued in the sight of Allah based on his or her Taqwa; it is not based on Salat or Saum which are merely tools for acquiring Taqwa.

6 Ummah: More Worships in Spiritual Dimension

Individual forms a building block of the society. Many of the spiritual worships discussed in chapter 5 had advantages for the individual worshipper as well as for the society in which he or she lives. In the current section we will consider additional worships in the spiritual dimension, whose focus is on the benefits to the society and the Muslim Ummah at large.

6.1 The purpose

While the individual seeks Allah, he or she simultaneously seeks fellowship with mankind. The success of the individual in one direction relates to the success in the other direction. In fact, it is impossible for an individual to seek out Allah while he or she is indifferent to the people. Similarly, it is impossible for an individual to genuinely reach out to mankind without also reaching out to Allah.

In the context of Quran, this is a relationship between the worship of Allah and the ethical behavior of the individuals in the Society, as in Quran 11:197: "For, never would thy Sustainer destroy a community for wrong [beliefs alone] so long as its people behave righteously [towards one another]" (M. Asad). It is therefore important that the people behave righteously among themselves as was discussed in sections 4.4.4 and 4.4.5.

The Ummah is entrusted with the task to establish what is right and abolish what is wrong, Quran 3:104: "Let there arise out of you a band of people inviting to all that is good enjoining what is right and forbidding what is wrong; they are the ones to attain felicity". This is to be done globally and internationally so that all people can know and worship Allah. Muslims will be held accountable for this task, collectively as the Ummah, Quran 22:78: "… It is He Who has named you Muslims both before and in this (Revelation); that the Apostle may be a witness for you and ye be witnesses for mankind! …". The task is formidable, and it is clear that the Ummah must lift itself to a position of strength in order to accomplish it on the international scene.

This worship at the level of the society is solely for the benefit of the society. It provides mankind the right environment to know Allah and to shun the evil notions. Quran values the approach based on observations, and invites us to analyze the cases of the past societies in the history of mankind, Quran 16:36: "For We assuredly sent amongst every People an apostle (with the Command) "Serve Allah and eschew Evil": of the people were some whom Allah guided and some on whom Error became inevitably (established). *So travel through the earth and see what was the end of those who denied* (the Truth)". Quran also provides us an example of the people who have done it successfully during the time of the Prophet (S), as described in Quran 3:110: "Ye are the best of peoples *evolved for mankind* enjoining what is right forbidding what is wrong and believing in Allah …". We can analyze these cases and apply the results to the society of our own place and our own time.

6.2 Worships at the level of the Ummah

Quranic worships described in this section are intended to develop the right organization among the Muslim countries. Quran prescribes the needed organizational principles to ensure that Muslims together may constitute a strong Ummah.

The Ummah has a mission to accomplish, as discussed above. Each Muslim individual must perform the "jihad" to ensure that this mission is successfully completed. This "jihad" is part of the worship of Allah at the level of the Ummah. Each individual must do his or her utmost to influence their government so that the Ummah becomes organized according to these Quranic principles. They must vehemently oppose all efforts of their government to selfishly flout these requirements of Quran. Many Kingships, Emirships, Oligarchies, and Militaries will setup nominal bodies of spineless non-representative individuals and claim that they have fulfilled Quranic requirements. It is not uncommon for these governments to bring onboard some religious Ulama who would issue religious Fatwas in favor of such government actions.

However, Quranic worships at the level of the Ummah are not asking for such trickery. Instead, they demand sincere dedication and relentless "jihad" from the rulers as well as on the part of the Muslim populace. It is time that the Muslim individuals educate themselves and learn to recognize tricknology. These have been played time and again, on the unsuspecting Muslim masses, by the self-seeking Muslim rulers as well as the non-Muslim predators, often time in collusion.

111

Specific Quranic requirements for the Muslim Ummah are discussed in the following subsections.

6.2.1 The unity

Quran clearly forbids disunity and groupings that weaken the community. It is prescribed that all Muslims must hold on to the "rope" of unity so that they do not disperse their efforts and energies. Following the guidance is important; however, it must be done preserving the unity of collective purpose. The result of following Allah's guidance manifests in unity and brotherhood. This leads people from hell to heaven. However, if the guidance is followed in such a way that the unity of collective effort is compromised then this is like being misguided. The metaphor of holding on to the "rope of Allah" must be observed in such a way that there is no divisiveness introduced among Muslims, that would compromise the position of Muslims with respect to the non-Muslims.

Muslims go to great lengths to observe the rituals. However, they sometimes do it in such a way that creates sectarian divisions that are prohibited by Quran. There can be no justification for so doing. Following the imams and leaders in a way that causes serious disunity among Muslims is in a manifest discord with Quran. Muslims insist that they must follow the Imams in spite of its sectarian consequences, which reminds one of the earlier Ummahs who went astray in following their forefathers blindly, as in Quran 43:22: "Nay! they say: "We found Our fathers following a certain religion and We do guide ourselves by their footsteps."" Some Muslims are so used to the sectarian divisions that most of them do not even realize that it is against Quran. Muslims live in a fool's paradise if they think that they can continue to defy Quran in this manner, and yet achieve salvation through observing the rituals alone.

Quran asks us to seek the straight path. We all profess that Islam is the straight path. Yet what we follow are divergent paths of various sects. This situation is not satisfactory.

Sects

Simple geometry tells us that, in order to determine a straight path, we must know two locations that are situated on that path. This requirement is easily met: one location being determined by Quran and the second location being determined by the Sunnah. How do Quran and Sunnah determine the strait path?

First thing to appreciate is that the straight path is not a narrow path; it is more like an extremely wide highway with so many lanes that the far-off lanes do not even appear to be on the same highway; yet they are on the same highway! How does that happen? The interpretation of Quran and the understanding of its message are not the same among all Muslims. This produces some dispersion to the notion of the straight path; making it a broad path. The understanding of the Sunnah and its meanings are even more diversified. This adds to the width of the path, making it a wide highway with dozens of lanes. Therefore, what we actually get is not a narrow path but a highway of extremely large width.

Two travelers on this highway are sometimes so far apart that it becomes difficult to recognize that they are actually on the same path.

But make no mistake, they are on the same highway on which you are. Do not fall for the optical illusion, never think even for a moment that they are deviant, lost, or on a separate path. Do not try to correct them under your own perceptions, they are assuredly fellow Muslims; greet them with love and brotherhood.

How to accomplish that? Short answer is to follow the rules of this highway. In order to avoid collisions on the highway of such immense dimensions, there have to be rules: the travelers must not encroach upon the lanes being used by the others; they must remain within the safe speed limits; and they must keep a safe distance from other travelers on this highway. Observing these safety rules is a way out of sectarianism: let others travel in their own lanes. Under the bad weather, when visibility is very low and the grip on the road very tenuous, extreme caution is needed, paying extra heed to the rules of the Islamic highway; because once the collisions happen, death and destruction are likely.

Different sects are like different lanes on the highway of the "straight path" of Islam. The reason for the sectarian strife is the lack of such rules, and a lack of willingness to observe the rules where they exist. The mental Hijrah that we discuss in this book is designed to rectify this situation; the unity of Muslims is of paramount importance.

The lack of rules for the highway of Islam is traceable to the space-time factor; the difficulty in implementing the localized traditions of a millennium ago in today's countries of myriad lifestyles on a global scale. Various sects were formulated at different places at various times, with different emphasis on living conditions, throughout the history. As there has been no mechanism to recognize and incorporate the vital role of different places and different times, and some have actually denied the need to incorporate such effects, the result is a discontinuity between the positions taken by the different sects. This makes a meaningful communication and dialogue very difficult. The isolation across discontinuities sometimes leads to hardened positions so that different sects start thinking of others with suspect integrity, and even suspecting their Muslim-ness; thereby losing sight of the fact that they are all fellow Muslims traveling on the very broad highway that Islam is today. Therefore, we need the mental Hijrah from a mindset that is content with an uncritical "taqlid" to a mind that learns, evaluates, and understands the purpose behind the Islamic teachings.

The problem of sectarianism has arisen because Muslims have neglected Allah's worships in the physical and ethical dimensions, as well as worships with respect to the glory of the Ummah. Rather, they have focused on a very small subset of what Allah requires of the Muslims; this subset consists of the ritualistic aspect concerning the five pillars, often with a blatant disregard towards their underlying objectives. Such attitude towards worship is highly unbalanced. The cure lies in paying attention to the worships that Muslims have neglected for centuries. These include the worship in the physical dimension, the worship in the ethical dimension, and the worship in the spiritual dimension at the level of the Ummah.

115

6.2.2 Collective decision making

Muslims are required to perform all their affairs using consultation mechanisms, as in Quran 42:38: "Those who hearken to their Lord and establish regular prayer; *who (conduct) their affairs by mutual Consultation*; who spend out of what We bestow on them for Sustenance". Please note how Quran inserts the requirement of consultation in the middle of the requirements for Salat and Zakat. This is the basis for conducting the affairs of the nation and the Ummah, as well as the affairs of Muslims at other levels of the society, see Quran 3:159: "...; and consult them in affairs (of moment). ...". Many regimes in the middle east are manifestly in discord with this Quranic requirement because they are despotic. It is the obligatory worship for all Muslims to struggle and establish a system of government that is based on the discussion and consultation for the purpose of making decisions. If Muslims do not perform this worship at the level of the Ummah, their ritualistic worships are proportionately without significance.

We used the term "proportionately", by which we mean the following. If some Muslims fail in this respect, yet most individuals attend to it and the government is therefore in accord with Quranic requirement, then the significance is diminished for the ritualistic worships of those who did not struggle to gear their government in the right direction. However, if most people fail in the worship at the level of the Ummah, such that, the government actually remains in discord with Quranic requirements, then it has more serious consequences. In the latter case, all those individuals who failed in the prescribed worships at the level of the Ummah would be held responsible on the

Day of Judgment. Their ritualistic worships are worthless, except those who did try and yet failed.

6.2.3 Mutual kindness and firmness

Muslims are required to be kind to one another. At the same time, they are required to stand firm together in the face of the enemy, as in Quran 48:29: "Muhammad is the Apostle of Allah; and those who are with him are strong against Unbelievers (but) compassionate amongst each other. ...".

This requirement of Quran is on one side and the sectarian behavior of Muslims is on the diametrically opposite side. Instead of being loving among themselves, they behave in an abominable way when they call each other "kafir" and cause many a violent sectarian strife.

At the same time, instead of being determined and able opponents for the enemies of Muslims they actually behave meekly towards them. In their ignorance, they even befriend the enemy. They provide the enemy with plenty of opportunity to divide Muslims and conquer them like a bunch of scattered tribes.

This was the condition of the Arabs at the time of the Prophet (S). The time has now come for a mental Hijrah, in the loving memory of our Prophet (S).

6.2.4 Alliances and collective strategy

The Muslim nations within the Muslim Ummah must be allies to each other, just as their enemies construct alliances, as is prescribed in Quran 8:73: "The unbelievers are protectors one of another: unless ye do this (protect each other) there would be tumult and oppression on earth and great mischief". If Muslims fail to develop alliances, it will lead to mischief and oppression on Earth. The failure of Muslims to get allied with one another will produce disaster for Muslims. The predicament of Muslims today is a living testimony to this situation that Quran has predicted.

The Muslim nations must join together in a well thought collective strategy in order to wash off the curse of disgrace and oppression from their present condition. It is the religious duty of every individual to demand of their governments that this Quranic requirement be respected among the Muslim nations. If the Muslim individuals do not do this "Jihad at large" they fail in an essential worship of Allah that Quran prescribes at the level of the Ummah. We emphasized that this collective failure of the Muslims cannot be compensated by excessive observance of the rituals like the Salat, Saum, Zakat and Haj. Muslims must pay attention to all worships that Quran prescribes at different levels and in different dimensions.

6.2.5 Uphold the righteousness and discourage the mischief

Muslims have a collective duty to uphold the good attitudes and actions, and discourage the bad ones, as in Quran 3:110: "Ye are the best of peoples evolved for mankind enjoining what is right forbidding what is wrong ...". They must do so globally throughout the world. This is an instruction to the entire Ummah. Its implications for the individual include an unceasing "Jihad at large" to see to it that the Ummah is capable of and actually does carry out this Quranic requirement. Not doing so is missing out at a worship at the level of Ummah.

Quran further instructs that there be a specialized group of people within the Ummah whose primary focus is to accomplish the establishment of righteousness and the abolishment of mischief, as in Quran 3:104: "Let there arise out of you a band of people inviting to all that is good enjoining what is right and forbidding what is wrong; they are the ones to attain felicity". Indeed, Muslims will be held accountable on the day of the Judgment with respect to the accomplishment of this assignment. This is an assignment to the entire Ummah, to be performed by well-trained personnel with adequate financing and proper organization; it does not mean a rag tag group of Tablighi Jamaat.

This worship must be understood in conjunction with the worships that require unity among Muslims, establishment of a government based on mutual discussions and consultation, and engineering of alliances among Muslim countries, as already discussed. The entire community gets itself properly organized and united. They develop alliances for mutual support. Then they posture to the non-Muslim communities from a position of strength. They work among them-selves and with non-Muslims in such a way that the good prospers and the bad decays. This is an exercise that the Ummah as a whole performs in the inter-national relations.

6.3 Recap

We started with the 'Book of Framework' that consists of the first two chapters. The chapter one opens the analysis with a description of the problem, an approach for a Quranic solution to that problem, the objectives for the solution approach, and finally the tools to be used for the solution implementation. We referred to the approach as the "Mental Hijrah", and also pointed out some pitfalls like those posed by the 'space-time' effect. In chapter 2 we presented the architecture for the framework needed for achieving the mental Hijrah. This architectural framework has three major modules. These are the worships of Allah in the three dimensions, namely physical, ethical, and spiritual.

Next, we presented the 'Book of Worships', which took an analytical view of the worships in the three dimensions. We discussed these individual modules of the architectural framework in chapters 23 through 6. We had to cover the spiritual dimension in two closely allied chapters, 5 and 6; inherently coupling the worships consisting of the five pillars with the worships at the level of the Ummah. Such intricate relationships become transparent when we use the 'Law of Shadows' presented in Theorem 2 on page 139. Such theorems are presented in the 'Book of Wisdom', which is absolutely vital to appreciate the deeper significance of Quranic guidance.

The first thing to firmly realize is that, none of the architectural modules is equivalent to the entire system. Therefore, the value of each module is ultimately determined by how well it plays its architectural role. The intermediate goals for the individual modules are fine, but they have their value only in so far as they contribute to the overall scheme. Thus, the conquest of the physical universe, the peace on Earth, and the five pillars are important only within this context. This architectural positioning of the Muslim activities is invaluable in order to keep the various activities in proper perspective, so that we neither underperform them nor over perform them. Further, we do not perform any of these activities in a naïve way such that they would hurt the very objectives they are intended to support. The worship of Allah in the three dimensions is inseparably intertwined with their objectives. Some of these points are recalled below.

- o Let us start with the worship in the physical dimension. It teaches us that it is vital to develop an understanding of the nature around us, which provides pointers to Allah. This understanding enables the conquest of the physical universe, and it provides one of the two components of the Taqwa.

- o Next let us consider the worship in the ethical dimension. The humans have a natural tendency to perform these worships because Allah breathed His "Ruh" into them. These worships keep the people honest, and produce a firm degree of commitment to adhere to the understanding that was acquired via the worships in the physical dimension. This commitment is also a foundation for the Taqwa. It is not possible to acquire Taqwa either without an understanding of the nature, or without a commitment to remain true to this understanding. Only in the presence of this Taqwa can a Muslim derive useful guidance from Quran for his or her final return to Allah. In the absence of Taqwa, Quran can provide no help whatsoever. The worships in the physical and ethical dimensions therefore constitute the starting point for the spiritual emancipation, and they also enable peace on Earth.

o   The worships in the spiritual dimension are tools for an accelerated enhancement of the Taqwa. The five pillars are very specific tools recommended for this purpose. As tools, they should always be viewed in relation to their objectives. In particular, none of the five pillars is an objective in itself.

Talking about the worship in the spiritual dimension, we wish to underscore that they have a collective component with respect to the Ummah. No spiritual emancipation is possible without this component. In Islam, the service to society enters at a fundamental level; it is neither an option nor an afterthought.

For example, there is a clear criterion with respect to the performance of the five pillars: if they fail to strengthen the Taqwa and the Ummah, they amount to no spiritual benefit. Should the observance of the five pillars cause sectarian strife, such that the activity actually hurts the Ummah, then this performance will cause a spiritual downfall in the eyes of Allah. It then does not qualify as worship; it actually becomes a grave sin that is worthy of grave punishment.

We emphasized above that the Taqwa is necessary for a person to derive guidance from the book of Allah. Those who approach this book without Taqwa do not find guidance. This looks like a chicken and egg situation, but it is not. There are other mechanisms to acquire

Taqwa. These are freely available via an exercise of the basic faculties, which all people are born with. These mechanisms are vital to bootstrap the acquisition of Taqwa. Once a "critical mass" of Taqwa has been acquired, the individual then possesses the correct disposition to be able to use Quran in order to accelerate the process. Quranic guidance can take this pursuit of the individual for Taqwa to such heights as are not possible otherwise.

In the 'Book of Wisdom' that follows, we will acquire a deeper understanding of the worship in the three dimensions. Such understanding is absolutely necessary to appreciate the intricate interdependencies, feedback mechanisms, and the lively dynamics between the modules of the architectural framework that we have discussed.

7 Book of Wisdom

The 'Book of Framework' and the 'Book of Worships' were discussed in the preceding chapters. These chapters built a framework to analyze the basic teachings of Islam in the light of what Quran explicitly states with respect to them. The framework views the Islamic teachings as a set of worships. These worships are performed in three different dimensions, namely the physical, ethical and spiritual. What is fundamental about the Islamic teachings is that all these three dimensions are important in so far as they combine to produce the structure that Islam aims to build at the level of an individual as well as at the level of the Ummah. If any of these dimensions is neglected or inadequately incorporated, the structure becomes weak, or can even crumble.

What is this structure that Islam aims to build? The answer derives from Quran itself. The objectives of the structure are twofold:

to build strong, free, and wise individuals with a high degree of Taqwa; and to use these individuals to constitute a strong, free, and wise Ummah with a high degree of Taqwa in its society.

Islam determines the objective, and tools to achieve that objective. The structure itself is left for the Ummah to evolve it, depending upon when it is needed and where it is needed. The structure is left flexible because its components depend upon where and when and the details of how. For instance, there was a time when the defense of the Ummah was built using swords and horses. But that has now evolved into a combination of military, air force, navy, and communications. The structure is left evolvable, but the objective remains the same. The tools are the worships in three dimensions, at the level of the individual and at the level of the Ummah. This book has elaborated these tools in detail.

The actual events in the life of the Prophet (S) confirm this objective, and demonstrate how to use the tools. The Prophet(S) used Quranic Hikmah in formulating the objective and in using the tools towards achieving the objective. This is the real Sunnah of the Prophet(S); it is not incorporated in the books of Hadith, because they are highly fragmented and highly incomplete, and they entirely miss out on the Hikmah that was ever present in everything the Prophet(S) said or did as well as did not say and did not do. The Sunnah is incorporated in the entire life of the Prophet, most of which is not recorded in the books of Hadith.

The need for the Hikmah is underlined in the individual Ayahs, though the Hikmah itself is not asserted in individual Ayahs; rather, it is left for the wise reader to infer it as the constant overarching theme that runs in the background of the individual Ayahs. The individual Ayahs make a coherently complete narrative only when understood in the light of the underlying overarching theme. An understanding of this theme is referred to as Hikmah of the Quran. Importance of Hikmah is clearly underlined in Quran.

Quran 2:129: "Our Lord! send amongst them an Apostle of their own who shall rehearse Thy Signs to them and instruct them in Scripture and Wisdom and sanctify them; for Thou art the Exalted in Might the Wise."

126

Quran 3:48: "And Allah will teach him the Book and Wisdom the Law and the Gospel".

Quran 2:269: "He granteth wisdom to whom He pleaseth; and he to whom wisdom is granted receiveth indeed a benefit overflowing; but none will grasp the message but men of understanding".

The best illustration of the Hikmah was embodied in the life of the Prophet(s) because he constantly used it in his teaching of the Quran, as in as in Quran 2:129. Hikmah was also granted to Isa(A), as in Quran 3:48. And Hikmah is granted to whosoever Allah blesses with it, as in Quran 2:269. While the book is more widely available, its Hikmah is available only to those wise people who really exert themselves in its understanding, as in Quran 2:269.

Most people lack the Hikmah of Quran. For instance, the narrations in the books of Hadith concentrate on the physical events and phraseology, while entirely missing on the Hikmah in them. The books of Hadith are very poor sources for the Hikmah of Quran, and therefore very poor representation of the Sunnah.

We need a framework in which to understand the global themes of Quran that contain the overarching wisdom (Hikmah); so that we can understand the individual Ayahs in that light; otherwise, there are possibly wild understanding of Quran using the linguistics, history, and cherry-picked Ahadith. The theorems presented in this 'Book of Hikmah' belong to this effort towards understanding the Hikmah. It seeks universal results that are global in nature in order to ensure the big picture that Islam intends. They are, therefore, a vital part of the integrated message of Quran. However, they do not derive on a local scale from one or more Quranic Ayahs. This distinction is the basis for differentiating the results presented in this Book of Hikmah from those presented earlier.

This book of Hikmah is just the beginning of research towards exploring the Hikmah of Quran. Without this, Muslims will continue to spend a disproportionate amount of energy in the five pillars of Islam and continue to lose sight of the structure that these pillars are intended to support.

The research results on the Hikmah of Quran will be referred to as the Theorems, because they are universally applicable to understand Quran. They are an attempt to verbalize Quranic wisdom.

Theorem 1 Taqwa is pre-requisite as well as the final criterion

Background

The concept of "Taqwa" is very fundamental in Islam. In spite of its importance, it has not been properly analyzed as a concept and a Quranic construct. This theorem elaborates its meanings and its position relative to other Quranic constructs.

In order to realize a perspective of Taqwa, we refer to Quran itself, as in Quran 2:2: "This Divine Writ – let there be no doubt about it – is [meant to be] a guidance for all the God-conscious" (M. Asad). We have taken the rendering of this verse into English by Mohammad Asad who points out that the conventional translation of "muttaqi" as "God-fearing" does not adequately render the positive content of this expression. This Quranic construct is more along the lines of being thoroughly aware of the all-presence of Allah and a total commitment to mold one's existence in the light of this awareness.

The formulation of this theorem analyzes the nature of Taqwa and defines its constituent elements.

Statement

Having asserted that Quran offers guidance to those who have Taqwa, Quran 2:2 has made Taqwa a pre-requisite for the seekers of guidance.

Quran has also made Taqwa the final criterion as to how successful one's efforts are to achieve closeness to Allah, as in Quran 49:13: "… Verily *the most honored of you in the sight of Allah is (he who is) the most righteous of you* (the one with most Taqwa). And Allah has full knowledge and is well acquainted (with all things)".

Taqwa is therefore of pivotal importance in the spiritual theory of Islam as formulated in Quran. It is a prerequisite to be able to use Quran as a source of guidance. It is also the ultimate criterion of success in the Eyes of Allah.

Quranic concept of Taqwa

Quranic construct of Taqwa is not something that can be understood from individual Ayahs. It must be gleaned from the totality of Quranic message, as a nugget of wisdom that Quran offers without explicitly verbalizing it.

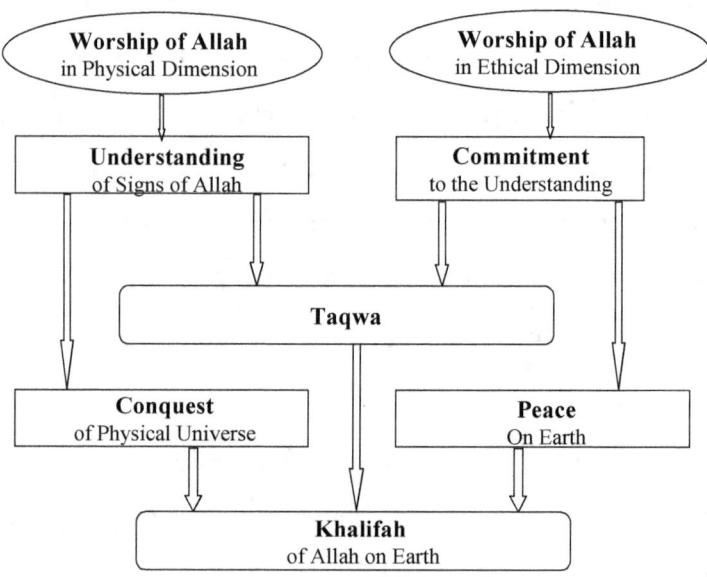

Figure 1 for Theorem 1: The worships in the physical and ethical dimensions bootstrap the Taqwa cycle.

The Taqwa is not the name of physical activities and ritualistic performances, though these are useful tools in the acquisition of Taqwa. On the other hand, Taqwa is the way one's body, mind and conscience are in total submission to the consciousness of Allah that one has acquired at any given stage of the voyage of one's life.

The accompanying figure illustrates how the Taqwa can be acquired and the central role this concept plays. Acquiring Taqwa is a continuous process. It works in cycles, as illustrated below.

1. We acquire some Taqwa through our contemplation on the Ayahs of Allah in nature (see chapter 3) and our worships in the ethical dimension (see chapter 4). Our physical faculties and our conscience are the principal tools at this stage.

2. The Taqwa acquired as described above fulfills the prerequisite in Quran 2:2. This enables us to seek guidance directly from Quran, in proportion to the degree of Taqwa that we have acquired. The guidance that we thus acquire from Quran increases our Taqwa by providing us a firmer understanding of the Signs of Allah and a firmer commitment (submission) to that understanding.

3. The guidance from Quran leads us towards the spiritual worships as discussed in chapters 5 and 6. For instance, we establish our communication with Allah (Salat) and we share our success with other people (Infaq); sharing makes Taqwa intrinsically a matter of passion for people, society, and the Ummah at large. The communication with Allah makes Taqwa inherently a matter of love for Allah. This can further increase

our Taqwa, again through an enhanced understanding and a higher level of commitment (submission).

This cycle continues till we finally meet Allah, as in Quran 2:46: "Who bear in mind the certainty that they are to meet their Lord and that they are to return to Him". Therefore, Taqwa at any given stage represents the state of preparedness for meeting Allah.

In addition, Figure 1 for Theorem 1 above makes the following statements.

Worship in the physical dimension has two consequences. It helps an understanding of the Ayahs of Allah in nature which produces understanding of these Ayahs. This understanding is roughly half of Taqwa. Another consequence is that, this understanding helps man to conquer the physical world which gives man physical powers.

Worship in the ethical dimension also has two consequences. First, it provides man with sincerity, and the ability to commit to the knowledge gained. This commitment is the other half of Taqwa. Understanding plus commitment to that understanding together produce Taqwa. The other consequence of worship in ethical dimension is the ability to achieve peace on earth, as well as some peace in one's heart.

Worships in these two dimensions help man become the Khalifah on earth because it provides man three essential things: the Taqwa which is the foundation, the physical conquest of natural phenomena, which is a practical need for being a Khalifah to produce peace on earth, which is the third thing.

You might wonder what do the worships in the spiritual dimension accomplish. They accomplish two objectives: first to strengthen the Taqwa of man, and second, they help produce a strong Ummah ready to establish peace for the entire mankind. This peace is superior in quality as it gives man a taste of spiritual living, and it gives the society a genuine peace on earth and peace in the hearts. More spiritual a society is, more they are deserving of playing the role of Khalifah on earth. Taqwa is a measure of spirituality in individuals as well as in societies.

As discussed in chapter 5, Angels play a crucial role to connect mankind with Allah. Being with Allah, like a flight from earth to heaven, is the real reward man derives from the worship in the spiritual dimension. We leave the details for our book on spirituality which is planned for publication soon.

Bootstrapping Taqwa

A degree of Taqwa must be present as a precondition in order to bootstrap the cyclical process described above. Once started, this process can be repeated throughout the entire life. The rate at which the process converges to its goal depends upon the degree of Taqwa with which the cyclic process was bootstrapped and the efficiency with which an individual and an Ummah use Quranic guidance in all three dimensions.

There is the question of bootstrapping the cyclical process to acquire Taqwa. That means to determine a mechanism to acquire an initial degree of Taqwa so that the cyclical process can get started. The figure illustrates how this start can be accomplished. It starts with a sincere application of the "worships" in the physical dimension, as were discussed in Chapter 3. These include an eagerness to learn, a keen and impartial observation, exercising one's wisdom to sincerely understand what was observed, and to internalize the knowledge so gained. The integrated result of these "worships" is an "Understanding" of the "Signs of Allah", as in Quran 20:114: "… say *"O my Lord! advance me in knowledge""*; and Quran 41:53: "In time We shall *make them fully understand Our messages* [through what they perceive] *in the utmost horizons* [of the universe] and *within themselves*, so that it will become clear unto them that this [revelation] is indeed the truth. [Still] is it not enough [for them to know] that thy Sustainer is witness unto everything" (M. Asad).

As the figure illustrates, there are at least two aspects to Taqwa, as was also discussed in section 4.3. First, one must have achieved a reasonable success at acquiring the "Understanding" of the Ayahs of Allah. Second, one must commit to these findings so that in one's thoughts, actions, and aspirations one must remain strictly committed to this "Understanding". This amounts to a total submission, as in Quran 2:208: "O ye who believe! enter into Islam whole-heartedly [willing total submission]; and follow not the footsteps of the Evil One; for he is to you an avowed enemy". This commitment can be achieved through the worships of Allah in the ethical dimension, as was discussed in chapter 4. The combined result of a profound understanding and a sincere commitment to it is the Taqwa. In other words, Taqwa is a function of two inputs, the understanding and the commitment to that understanding. It derives from worships in the physical and ethical dimension. Without it, no guidance obtains from Quran, and one remains unprepared for the worships in spiritual dimension.

Levels of Taqwa

Of course, the Taqwa is neither monolithic nor binary in its nature. People differ in the level of their understanding of the "Ayahs" and also in their commitment to this understanding. Therefore, people have different degrees of Taqwa to bootstrap the Taqwa cycle as described above. The understanding of the "Ayahs" via the natural phenomenon can genuinely cover a broad spectrum of possibilities. Some people can be less apt at it than others, and one's education and training can be a significant factor. A more uniform aspect of Taqwa is one's commitment to one's understanding; even though here too the sincerity in one's approach can broadly vary based on the values of the society. This view allows a wide variety of possibilities for Taqwa. These possibilities are exemplified by the levels of Taqwa listed below.

Level 0: An individual may have little understanding of the natural phenomena and (s)he may have little or no commitment to whatever little understanding (s)he has. This may be the case of a person who is not especially knowledgeable or sincere.

Level 1: A person may have less than deep understanding of the Ayahs of Allah but her/his commitment to this understanding may be very superior because of the sincerity factor. This may be the case with a sincere person who is not particularly knowledgeable.

Level 2: An individual may have very profound understanding of the natural phenomenon but (s)he may be less than true to her/his understanding. This may be the case with some scientists who understand the Ayahs but are less committed to use their understanding for the benefit of all mankind.

Level 3: Finally, a person may have very profound understanding of natural phenomena and may also have the highest degree of commitment to use this understanding to the benefit of all. This may be the case of a scientist who is also a saint. Some learned Sufis might fall in this category.

Please note that we have not included the case where an individual has no understanding but has a deep commitment. Quranic concept of Taqwa leaves no room for it: for if Quranic prescriptions for worship in the physical dimension are followed, the individual cannot remain without understanding even when there is no formal education involved. This case of commitment to an understanding that does not exist corresponds to dogmatic behavior. There is no place for dogmas in Islam. As discussed in Chapter 3 one always keeps an open mind for further and more profound understanding, and one continues to actively strive for understanding.

There is one final remark with respect to the figure above. It shows the Ummah established at the position of the Khalifah of Allah on Earth. The Ummah must fulfill three requirements for this purpose. First and foremost, they must have Taqwa at the level of the individual as well as the Ummah. This is essential to establish the virtues and purge the vices, as well as to protect the Ummah with the Rahmah from Allah so that the Ummah does not behave as a secular super-power would. Second comes the Peace on Earth. The Ummah must be in a position of strength so as to establish a just peace. The position of strength that the Ummah must acquire includes strength in the ethical and spiritual dimensions, as well as the strength in the physical dimension. This brings us to the third requirement for the Ummah in order to qualify for the position of the Khalifah on Earth. This is the "Conquest" of the physical universe using the scientific research and discovery.

Corollary 1:   No human can judge the Taqwa of another person.
As a corollary, it follows that the Taqwa is strictly between the individual and Allah. This is so at least in three aspects as stated below.

- First, we may judge some one's knowledge by comparing it to our own knowledge: however, Allah is the only One Who has all knowledge and therefore shall judge our knowledge correctly.
- Second, the internal commitment of an individual to the knowledge (s)he possesses is not known to anyone except the individual and Allah, Who knows what we reveal and what we conceal. Therefore, Allah alone can judge our commitment.
- Third, there is the issue of the formula to combine the knowledge and the commitment, in order to generate Taqwa from its two ingredients. Nobody has the exact formula because nobody understands the "knowledge" and "commitment" adequately. However, Allah does understand these concepts perfectly, He can precisely determine their presence in the case of an individual, and combine the two measurements "justly".

Therefore, it is not only impossible for a human to judge the "Taqwa" of somebody else, to attempt to do that is an exercise in ignorance and arrogance. Some might argue that judging someone else for Taqwa amounts to blasphemy because only Allah can do that.

Theorem 2   The Law of Shadows

Background

Acquisition of Taqwa takes place in terms of the two practices, namely Salat and Infaq, as in Quran 2:3: "Who believe in the Unseen are steadfast in prayer and spend out of what We have provided for them".

These two are apparently very different type of worships. Salat is a in spiritual dimension, while Infaq concerns the people in ethical dimension. However, they represent two facets of the same reality. The difference is only superficial. In other words, the two worships in two different dimensions are just two reflections of the reality.

This is an expression of a larger law that operates as an interface and feedback mechanism between the worships in different dimensions. We will call it the Law of Shadows after Quran 13:15: "Whatever beings there are in the heavens and the earth do prostrate themselves to Allah (acknowledging subjection) with good will or in spite of themselves: so do their shadows in the mornings and evenings".

In the current discussion of Salat and Infaq, the law of shadows represents an interface between the spiritual dimension and the ethical dimension. The result of this interface is a feedback mechanism that establishes a kind of "equivalence" between the spiritual and ethical worships. Quran uses such an "equivalence principle" when it recommends that, in certain cases, a failure to observe the spiritual worships may be compensated for by performing appropriate ethical worships.

o The inability to fast may be compensated by feeding the poor, as in Quran 2:184.

o When a person cannot keep his or her oath with Allah, (s)he may compensate for it by performing the ethical worships like feeding or clothing the indigent persons or freeing a slave. If the ethical worships cannot be performed because of the limitation of resources, then the failure to keep oath may be compensated by fasting for three days, as in Quran 5:89.

It is a reflection of this law that Quran hardly ever talks about the Salat without at the same time also talking about the Zakat. The spiritual worships produce closeness to Allah, which also brings the individual close to the people. This is a very profound aspect of Quranic approach. It makes spirituality manifest by making it physically observable through its "interfaces" with the ethical dimension. These interfaces are implemented through the shadows of spiritual worships that are cast in the ethical dimension.

Statement

The "Law of Shadows" states that the things come in canonical pairs, as in Quran 36:36: "Glory to Allah Who created in pairs all things that the earth produces as well as their own (human) kind and (other) things of which they have no knowledge". Each spiritual accomplishment has a canonical entity in the observable world that it pairs with in the canonical sense. One entity in the canonical pair is regarded as the shadow of the other. Thus, each spiritual accomplishment has an observable entity as its shadow in the observable world in physical or ethical dimensions.

The two entities that comprise a canonical pair are treated on equal footing. It is not that one is the primary object and the other is its shadow: the role of the object or the shadow can be played by either entity in the canonical pair. They can freely interchange their roles with respect to one another.

It is clear from the above discussion that an object cannot and will not exist without its shadow.

Examples

Some of the canonical pairs are exemplified below.

o Closeness with Allah AND closeness with humanity form a canonical pair.

The law of shadows states that closeness with Allah will imply closeness with people, and vice versa. It also implies that an object will not exist without its shadow. Thus, if someone is close to Allah, this spiritual emancipation will manifest itself in his or her compassionate behavior towards the people. According to this law it would not be credible for some individual to claim closeness to Allah while (s)he behaves inappropriately with the people.

o The five pillars AND the goals with respect to the Ummah form a canonical pair.

The law of shadows states that the observance of the five pillars of Islam must reflect itself in a proportionate strengthening of the position of the Ummah with respect to the non-Muslim nations. In particular, the law states that an observance of the five pillars of Islam in such a way that hurts the position of the Ummah is an invalid attempt at spiritual worship.

    o   Spiritual worship AND the ethical worship form a canonical pair.

The law implies that a good observance of the five pillars of Islam must manifest itself in the form of an exceptional ethical behavior. It was in this manner that the Prophet (S) had an exemplary ethical conduct, as in Quran 68:4: "And thou (standest) on an exalted standard of character". In particular, if someone seems to persistently observe the spiritual acts but does not treat his or her parents according to how Quranic ethics require (discussed in chapter 4) then such observance of spirituality is of doubtful value.

In general, a spiritual act with its observable shadow missing has a suspect validity. One object of a canonical pair cannot be realized without the other. In particular, the spirituality will not exist without its ethical manifestations and its desired effects on the position of the Ummah.

Following specific observations are made in relevance to Muslims today. They can be regarded as corollaries to the Law of Shadows.

Corollary 1   Spirituality must accompany good ethics.

The spiritual worships form a canonical pair with the ethical worships. Hence the spirituality will not exist without a visibly enhanced ethical conduct. Since the two entities in a canonical pair are on equivalent footing, the ethical worships and the spiritual worships will each enhance the other.

The spiritual worships symbolize the acts of an individual in seeking Allah. The ethical worships symbolize the acts of an individual in seeking humanity. The law of shadows links these two worships in an inseparable way so that neither can exist without the other. Further, the success of the individual in seeking Allah may be accurately measured by the ethical behavior of that individual. The closeness with Allah and the compassion for the humanity form a canonical pair. A claim of closeness to Allah must therefore cast its shadow by displaying a genuine warmth and compassion for the people.

Corollary 2   Observance of the five pillars must strengthen position of the Ummah.

The five pillars of Islam form a canonical pair with the strength of the Ummah with respect to the non-Muslim nations. A quantitative measure of the effectiveness of observing the five pillars is therefore provided by the degree to which the Muslim Ummah stands strengthened compared to others. Hence these five pillars must never be so observed that the strength of the Ummah is compromised.

Corollary 3   Sectarian behavior is un-Islamic

Sectarianism is a behavior, as discussed in section 6.2.1. Its impact on the position of the Ummah with respect to the non-Muslim nations is to cause disunity and weakness of the Ummah. This effect is an unacceptable "shadow" for any valid spiritual activity. It follows that the sectarian behavior is caused by invalid activities conducted in the guise of spiritualism.

Theorem 3   Rituals are not objectives

Background

It is often perceived that Islamic rituals are end objectives in themselves. Hence there is a disproportionate amount of emphasis on carrying out rituals like the Salat and Haj. This notion is mistakenly derived from an abundance of the mentions of Salat and Zakat in Quran. As Theorem 1 states, the Taqwa is the real objective. The performance of the rituals (discussed in chapters 5 and 6) is useful only as tools to acquire Taqwa.

Statement

The performance of the rituals does not automatically add to Taqwa: Taqwa is the objective; rituals are not the objective, rather they are the tools to acquire the objective.

If the rituals are performed and yet they do not contribute to the Taqwa, then it is as if they were not performed. Such observance of rituals is useless. If the observance of the rituals is actually detrimental to Taqwa, then such observance of rituals is sinful.

Discussion

How do we know if the observance of rituals is adding to Taqwa or not? The law of shadows as discussed in Theorem 2 on page 139 is indeed very useful in this context. We examine the ritualistic spiritual worship and its canonical pair in the ethical dimension. We look for the shadow of each ritualistic activity. The shadow reveals itself in the conduct of the worshipper; or the impact of the activity on the other people, the society and the Ummah. We examine the effect of the ritual observance on the following entities: the worshipper, other individuals, the society and the Ummah, and possibly other entities. We examine the beneficent effects of the ritualistic activity on each of these entities as well as its negative impacts on each of these entities. Following are some interesting cases.

- If the ritualistic activity is beneficent to at least one entity and it has no negative effects on any entity, then the ritual is contributing positively to the Taqwa.

- If the ritualistic activity has no beneficent effect on any entity but it does have harmful effects on at least one entity, then it is most plausibly a sinful activity under the guise of a spiritual ritual.

- The most difficult case is the one in which the ritual has both beneficent and harmful impacts on the entities. In that case we need to take a weighted-sum of the benefits and the harmful effects. While the determination of the weight factors is extremely difficult, the following are almost self-evident: the weight for the society is larger than the weight for the individual; and the weight for the Ummah is the highest.

Corollary 1: Rituals must support their objectives

Since rituals are not objectives in themselves, they cannot be performed without an explicit evaluation as to how well they enhance the objectives for which they are intended. While the eventual objective of all Islamic rituals is to enhance the Taqwa, as discussed above, they also have intermediate objectives.

146

Each ritual is designed to support explicit intermediate objectives. Quran spells these objectives out, as was illustrated in chapter 5. However, further research is very much needed to explore these intermediate objectives, map them on the individual rituals, and prioritize them.

Corollary 2:   All the rituals must be performed in a balanced way
The rituals are only as important as the objectives for which they are designed. Therefore, all the rituals must be performed so that all the objectives are met. Further, they should be performed to a degree that produces an optimal integrated result, appropriately combining the individual objectives towards accomplishing the overarching Islamic goals. This requires a balanced view towards all the rituals such that they are neither over performed nor under performed. All rituals should be performed, and they should be performed with an assigned priority in such a way that the overarching objectives are optimally realized.

In particular, an extreme behavior (see section 6.2) is not permissible in the performance of the rituals.

8 Suggestions for further research

Research is part of a Muslim's Jihad at large. It is also an effort to understand one's religion and to advance in the spiritual dimension. As the Jihad is needed in the battlefield, so it is needed in these fields as well.

First, we need the research to further develop the architectural framework that is presented in this book. This framework is needed to understand the various Islamic teachings and activities within Quranic grand scheme of things. This understanding is via an appreciation of their proper position in the framework as well as their mutual interfaces and feedback loops.

Second, we need research in the physical dimension that was detailed in chapter 3. Here we will take the opportunity to say more on the topic. Even though we shall refrain from discussing explicit scientific programs, however, it is important to realize that Quran is an excellent motivator with respect to the questions of scientific import.

Third, we need research in the spiritual dimension. We have provided some examples of this research, in the form of the three theorems already given in the 'book of wisdom'. Here we will take the opportunity to make further suggestions regarding the topics of spiritual research that we deem useful within the context of the mental Hijrah.

Fourth, we need research in organizational matters.

8.1 Research in framework

This book provides some starting momentum to develop a systematic framework for making choices and decisions in matters relating to Islam and Muslims, using the tools that Allah has given us. New and unfamiliar situations continue to surface as a consequence of the dynamic nature of life, offering new opportunities and new challenges. In comparison with situations encountered by the early Muslims, the space and time considerations of what, where, and when complicate approaches to analysis and action. The framework that we seek is required to help analyze these issues in a coherent manner, and to deal with the divergence of different understandings on the same issue, and moving forward to actions. In particular, one of the objectives is to move away from the opinion-based approach that has been used by Muslims after the death of the Prophet, and more dramatically after the era of the Caliphs. One purpose of this research is to do away with the opinion-based approach; and, instead, to adopt a logical framework that would allow meaningful dialogue, collective decision making, and collective approaches in the service of Ummah.

In this book we have laid a foundation for the needed framework. We have specified the basic criteria for the sources of guidance that form the foundation of such a framework. We have also given examples of some potential pitfalls like the space-time effects of what, where, and when. Using these building blocks, we suggested a framework that describes the human activities in terms of the worships of Allah in three critical dimensions. We explored the inter relationships between these worships and their relative roles with respect to one another. We discussed the objectives for each type of worship, showed how these worships complement one another in enhancing the Taqwa, and discussed how Taqwa relates to individual's closeness to Allah, as well as the strength of the Ummah.

This research effort should remain focused on addressing the causes that keep hurting the Muslim Ummah today. The focus should not be at endless discussions but to arrive at pragmatic solutions that can be acted upon; these can be improved as we gain experience.

The focus can be sharpened, by using the law of shadows as described in Theorem 2 on page 139. The intangible theological and spiritual aspects can be efficiently handled by examining their observable shadows.

8.1.1 Priority research topics

The framework that I have proposed in this book needs to be critically examined by the world-wide Muslim forums. The result of this research activity would be a modified and evolved framework; or even a completely new one. Some aspects of this examination are described in the following subsections.

Fundamental Inputs

We need to agree as to what are the fundamental building blocks for the framework. The building blocks that I have proposed are the three sources of guidance, as discussed in chapter 1.

Although these sources of guidance are fundamental, their detailed meanings are not unambiguous. This is especially true regarding the Sunnah of the Prophet, as was pointed out in section 05.2. It would

151

take a gigantic research effort to resolve these ambiguities. However, it surely can be done within the context of our space-time.

The objectives

We need to formulate a fairly complete set of high-level objectives for the framework.

I have used the following two objectives as fundamental to the Islamic teachings.

- To build strong, free, and wise individuals with a high degree of Taqwa as was discussed in chapters 3 through 5.
- The above individuals must build a strong Ummah as was explained in chapter 6.

Two other requirements that I have imposed on this framework are as follows.

- The framework seeks to get rid of the harmful impacts of the sectarian strife in Islam. In fact we require of the framework that the multiplicity of approaches towards an issue, that exists between the various schools of thought among Muslims, must be usable as an asset.
- The framework seeks to reinforce the worships of Allah in those dimensions that Muslims have neglected over centuries. These include the worships in the physical dimension (see chapter 3) and those at the level of the Ummah (see chapter 6).

The overarching themes

The detailed framework that emerges from our effort needs to encompass all the overarching themes that run implicitly in Quranic narrative. Some examples of these themes are provided as theorems in the 'Book of Wisdom'. However, much more research is needed to formulate a complete set of theorems, which are both necessary and sufficient.

Such themes serve to define the details of the architectural modules within the framework, as well as the interfaces and the feedback mechanisms between these modules.

Detailed Framework

I have proposed a framework, as described in chapter 2 and elaborated in chapters 3 through 6. This framework needs to be evaluated in many ways, in the light of the fundamental inputs, the objectives, and the overarching themes as described above.

o This framework needs to be tested against the objectives that it is required to meet, closely examining the extent to which the objectives are met.

o The framework also needs to be evaluated for its treatment of the fundamental inputs and the overarching themes. This includes an examination of how well the framework incorporates the fundamental inputs, and a test of the depth and the rigor with which it employs the fundamental inputs to generate the output to optimally respond to the challenges and the opportunities experienced by the Muslims and the Ummah in the space-time of today.

These tests imply an examination of the constituent modules of the framework, as well as their inter relationships. Specifically, we need to closely scrutinize the details with respect to the worships of Allah in

the three dimensions. The examination of the inter relationships between these modules means that we need to scrutinize how the
worship in each dimension complements and strengthens one another
in order to meet the objectives in the light of the overarching Quranic
themes.

8.1.2 Other research topics

In order to perform the research described in section 8.1.1 above, we
need to properly grasp Quranic message. In this section we provide
some seed ideas for grasping the message clearly.

Hierarchy of Quranic statements

Quran says that some verses are clear with respect to their meanings,
purpose, and scope etc. While there are some verses that have
ambiguities. Quran 3:7: "He it is Who has sent down to thee the Book:
in it are verses basic or fundamental (of established meaning); they are
the foundation of the Book: others are allegorical. But those in whose
hearts is perversity follow the part thereof that is allegorical seeking
discord and searching for its hidden meanings but no one knows its
hidden meanings except Allah and those who are firmly grounded in
knowledge say: "We believe in the Book; the whole of it is from our
Lord"; and none will grasp the Message except men of understanding".

The Ayah states that ambiguities exist, and only wise people will
understand their meanings. There is a strong need to separate these
verses with ambiguities and clearly catalogue them. This should be a
relatively easy matter, but one that carries a great deal of significance
in avoiding ambiguities.

There is a further hierarchy even within the set of verses that are deemed clear of ambiguity. This hierarchy is with respect to the purpose and scope, as well as how they fit into a framework of overarching themes of Quran. This hierarchy needs to be investigated, understood, and documented in a standardized manner; and the processes of such investigations are themselves topics of further research. Some of these will evolve as the experience base grows so there is no need to resolve them thoroughly before getting started.

There are verses in Quran that represent Universal truths, and there are those that refer to particular situations. They form different echelons of the hierarchy. The understanding of such a hierarchy is an initial step in understanding Quranic message. Some aspects of this process were discussed in section 5.2 on page 071.

Generalization of specific verses

Research is needed to understand the purpose and scope of those Quranic Ayahs that were revealed in response to specific incidents during the history of the revelation. As a first step these verses need to be clearly identified and catalogued.

Meanings of ambiguous verses

The ambiguous verses are part of the book. The intention is not to imply that no attempt should ever be made to understand them. The intention is to make such efforts with extra care and homework, and to explicitly guard against the possibility of deriving a misleading message from them. Great wisdom is needed to interpret them, but they are meant to be interpreted.

155

Such verses should be researched and reported in standard publications. If the efforts continue with persistence, we will benefit from the inspiration that these verses embody.

Role of the Sunnah

As was discussed in section 5.2, a gigantic amount of research is needed to understand the Sunnah as a source of guidance. Some specific issues to be researched include the following.

- o The definition of the Sunnah
- o Definition of the sources of the Sunnah
- o Identification of some sources of Sunnah
- o Critical evaluation of the sources of Sunnah
- o Better organization and presentation of the information contained in the commonly adopted sources of Sunnah
- o Methods of organizing the material of the Sunnah in a hierarchical framework with respect to the guidance embedded in the material and its import for Muslims in the space-time of today.
- o Development of the standardized hierarchies for the Sunnah material
- o Methods of using the Sunnah in making decisions
- o Methods and procedures for the simultaneous use of the human intellect, Quran, and the Sunnah in the resolution of an issue facing Muslims today

Mechanism

Muslims need to evolve a set of institutions and a tradition of collective effort in order to accomplish the needed research. Research is needed to organize the effort, the process to follow, and to properly treat the research results. The treatment of the research results includes their publication, standards of refereeing and criticism, rules of the applicable logic, and standards for applying the research results. Further details are provided in chapter 8.4.

These are formidable tasks. However, they are not showstoppers. We need to get going, and the road will get easier as we gain experience.

8.2 Research in science

Quran prescribes the worship of Allah in the physical dimension, as was discussed in detail in chapter 3. As discussed there, this worship is the scientific research with a twist: in addition to the conventional research, it has an eye towards the acquisition of Taqwa. Please note that the reverse is not true, that is, the scientific research per se is not necessarily the worship of Allah; only when the research leads to Taqwa, does it qualify as the worship of Allah.

The research in sciences is necessary for many reasons. First and foremost is the reason that Allah prescribes it in Quran. There are also other reasons for it. It can lead to Taqwa and a greater love for Allah. Also, it is necessary in order to accomplish the "conquest" of the physical universe as Allah has ordained for mankind.

On the practical grounds, the scientific research is necessary because it places tremendous powers at the disposal of mankind.

157

Without this power Muslims cannot provide an effective deterrence for those who are determined to destroy the peace on Earth, as was discussed in section 4.6.

We shall not dwell on the specific issues of science and technology. On the other hand, we shall emphasize Quranic attitude towards science, focusing on the needs for the purpose of the mental Hijrah.

The individual, the nation, and the Ummah must all focus on Quranic worships in the physical dimension, in a coherent manner so as to develop and excel programmatically. In executing the scientific research programs, the focus must be to do it with a Quranic mindset. This will enable the Ummah to influence the world from a position of strength, and to provide an effective and credible deterrence for those who spoil the world peace.

8.2.1 Priority research topics

As discussed in detail in chapter 3, Quran requires Muslims to inculcate scientific attitudes and use them to observe the signs of Allah. Such signs are scattered all over the physical universe (nature).

The scientific attitudes include a genuine desire for knowledge, a keen observation to acquire knowledge, a non-superstitious attitude towards the observations, and a non-dogmatic analytical approach to theorize the observed phenomena.

As discussed in chapter 3, when the signs of Allah are understood, they open up the heart and mind as a seeker (Salik). This is the way to Taqwa, which opens the heart and mind for guidance and inspiration. At the same time, the understanding of these signs opens the doors towards harnessing the powers of nature for our advantage in order to establish good and abolish evil (see section 6.2). When accomplished, it makes us the Khalifah on this Earth. There are therefore two tasks at hand for Muslims today.

- o To establish Quranic mindset towards the sciences, as was discussed in chapter 3.
- o To establish programs at the level of the Ummah, in order to become the Khalifah on this Earth.

As we discussed in chapter 6, a major goal of Islam is to establish the Muslim Ummah in a position that it can influence the world affairs in a decisive way. The goal is to work to establish what is good and abolish what is evil. This cannot be done in the world as it is, except from a position of strength (Quran 8:60).

The best example is provided by the Prophet (S). He used the best physical means available in his space-time, using the sciences of discipline, psychology, trade, diplomacy, political treaties, war, and peace. This approach helped the scattered tribes of the West coast of the Arabian peninsula to turn themselves into the superpower of the world. This is an example that is ready to repeat itself for Muslim Ummah today.

The Prophet (S) paid a keen attention to the sciences. Subsequently, the excellence in sciences remained an important priority for all the Muslim states and dynasties. Even during the days of relative decadence, the importance of knowledge and sciences was not ignored. However, Muslims gradually lost their zeal for knowledge. Instead of being the guardians and producers of knowledge, Muslims of today have merely become its consumers. One cannot correctly consume what one does not properly understand. The producers of the knowledge understand it the best, and they derive the most effective benefits from it. This circumstance has been promoted by the events of the colonial era. Muslims endured a continued inhumane treatment at the hands of the foreign forces. They started to equate the tyranny of the colonial powers with the instruments that they used for suppression and oppression. The instruments of injustice and occupation were enabled by the scientific research so that the science itself started to be viewed as anti-Muslim! Many Ulama started to justify this impression and caused an un-Islamic partition of knowledge into religious and secular, see section 3.4.

Muslims can now see through the haze of confusion. It has been only over the past century that Muslims have lost their proper place in the world. This is a short duration compared to the long period of time during which they effectively determined the direction in which the winds of the world would blow. Muslims in this new century are ready to claim their rights and privileges. They are ready to employ the scientific research in the service of the Ummah, as the earlier Muslims had also done. It is a part of the mental Hijrah.

Yes, the best example is that of the Prophet (S). It will, however, do us no good if we do not understand it, and use it to guide ourselves towards the possibilities, and caution ourselves against pitfalls. We must factor in the space-time effects while doing this exercise. If the Prophet (S) used the bow and arrow, it does not mean that we use it in a naïve worthless imitation of his example. We must understand the essential principles of the global strategy behind the actions of the Prophet (S), rather than imitating the detailed procedures that were valid only in their space-time context.

8.2.2 Other research topics

Quran makes abundant references to the physical phenomena in their capacity as the signs of Allah. These descriptions in Quran display an amazing subtlety and accuracy. As was discussed in section 3.4, these statements were far ahead of the state of development of the sciences, at the time they were originally made. As they were addressed to a humanity that was scientifically quite primitive, compared to the scientific developments today, they are often made in a subtle allegorical style. Quran itself refers to this circumstance in Quran 3:7.

Some examples are discussed by writers such as Maurice Bucaille (ISBN 0-89259-010-6). However, such discussions are after the fact. The descriptions in Quran are, however, much more powerful than such after-the-fact assertions can exemplify. To use Quranic power, we need to get serious, because Muslims do not have the right attitude to appreciate the power in the words of the Creator. They make little attempt to comprehend them and some pay little heed to the nuggets of knowledge that can be inspiring to a scientist.

The first research effort must be to correct this attitude.

One attitude comes from those who have neglected the worships of Allah in the physical dimension. They have no urge at deciphering the "signs" of Allah and are ever willing to "blindly accept" whatever may be stated in the name of Islam. Another attitude comes from Muslims who are professional scientists. Many depend on the trends that are established in Euro-America, and in their practice of the scientific profession, they do not regard the statements in Quran as worth being pondered upon. Both these attitudes are erroneous. The Ulama must acquire a respect for the value in the scientific attitudes and practices: and the Muslim scientists need to develop programs that resonate with the interests and the priorities of the Ummah.

8.3 Research in spirituality

Some folks might view the term "research in spirituality" as an oxymoron. This is the result of a common misunderstanding.

Quran asks us to perform the worship in the physical dimension, which amounts to the scientific research and leads to the scientific attitudes, as was discussed in chapter 3. However, the methodology of research and the scientific attitude is not inculcated for purely physical purpose. This is the Hikmah in Quran that (re)uses these mundane human skills also for the spiritual emancipation.

Admittedly the spiritual dimension is different from the physical dimension, as was discussed in section 5.2. The laws that operate in the spiritual dimension are different, as are the phenomena that manifest themselves in the spiritual dimension. The same attitude of "research" based on learning, observing, theorizing, and internalizing is, however, valid in the physical dimension as well as in the spiritual dimension. That is a Hikmah why Quran emphasizes these skills.

Research in the physical dimension as well as the spiritual dimension consists of observing, understanding and knowing the

Ayahs of Allah. In the spiritual dimension, the Ayahs of Allah are of a spiritual nature. Quran has examples of Ayahs in the spiritual dimension, just as it does contain examples in the physical dimension. The ritualistic spiritual practices discussed in chapters 5 and 6 are the tools for the spiritual research. They let us experience the phenomena in the spiritual universe through physical activities. The spiritual research consists of the usual cycle of progressively deeper experiences followed with ever more illuminating analysis. As discussed in Theorem 1 on page 129, this research is based on Taqwa with respect to the ability to experience spiritual phenomena as well as the capability to observe and analyze them. We need to find a systematic way to share the results of this spiritual research so that the sum total of human spiritual experience may grow cumulatively.

As discussed above, the process of spiritual research is similar to the research in the physical dimension, in many ways. Both types of research consist of the profound knowledge of the Ayahs of Allah using the same basic attitudes consisting of experiencing and analyzing.

However, there are also important differences. For instance, the spiritual research is impossible without Taqwa, while it is not so for the physical research. The laws in the spiritual dimension are well defined, though they are of an entirely different nature compared to the laws in the physical dimension. These laws are stated in Quran, but considerable research effort is needed to identify them, formulate them, and explore their consequences. An example of this process is provided by the Theorems in the Book of Hikmah.

163

Islam does not separate spirituality from government and takes a unified and holistic view of life. The spirituality in the people does not bloom without fulfilling the collective worship towards the Ummah, and the "world peace" does not bloom without the spirituality in its people. The two are intertwined to produce the beauty that Islam is.

The research in the spiritual dimension must be able to clearly differentiate between the form and the reality. The spiritual emancipation is a degree of closeness with Allah, which is not a physical thing in itself. However, the tools to attain this emancipation are physical things. Examples of the tools are the prayer, fasting, charity, pilgrimage, and other forms of meditation. These are all physical things to be used as tools for spiritual emancipation. The value of these tools holds only to the extent that they help attain closeness with Allah. The tools themselves are not spirituality, nor do they signify closeness with Allah.

The closeness with Allah does however manifest itself through the law of shadows discussed in Theorem 2 on page 139. This situation is a great help. It allows the differentiation of the spiritual people from those who fake spirituality for worldly gains.

The law of shadows also helps us achieve higher degrees of spirituality. We can observe the effectiveness of our prayer and fasting etcetera in the mirror of the law of shadows, and improve our spiritual efforts by observing how their shadows behave.

A good example of research in the spiritual dimension is provided by the three theorems discussed in the 'Book of Wisdom'. It also provides an example of how to document the results of the spiritual research, and how they may be shared via journals, articles, and books. Of course, we need to establish such journals and publications, as well as the human organization necessary for such forums. Here, we limit our discussion to the basic requirements of the mental Hijrah, and not embark upon exploring the work of the Sufis which is relevant to this discussion.

Another example of the spiritual research is provided by the discussion in section 5.2, concerning the mechanisms by which a spiritual prayer may have impact on the results in physical dimension.

8.3.1 Priority research topics

The topics of research that are most urgent are those concerning the five pillars. These were discussed in chapter 5, but a lot more research is needed to find their deeper spiritual meanings, advantages, and consequences. This can easily be done by paying a critical attention to the statements in Quran concerning these rituals. Important thing is to get started in a systematic and organized manner.

The law of shadows discussed in Theorem 2 on page 139 is of great help. We can incrementally sharpen the effectiveness of the five pillars in achieving the goals by observing the shadows of these spiritual worships as they manifest in the lives of the individuals as well as the position of the Ummah among the nations of the world. The individual conduct and the position of the Ummah are complementary to each other, and Islam uses them in this capacity. Therefore, it is important to be able to fine-tune the role and flavor of the rituals, according to the challenges that the Ummah faces as well as the opportunities that exist for the Ummah in the space-time of today. The Prophet (S) certainly used these pillars in this manner.

8.3.2 Other research topics

Following are good candidates to conduct research in the spiritual dimension. One goal of this research is to make the issues sufficiently clear to save the Ummah from the harmful effects of sectarianism, discussed in section 6.2, and clarified in Quran:

> Quran 30:32: "Those who split up their Religion and become (mere) Sects each party rejoicing in that which is with itself!"

> Quran 6:159: "As for those who divide their religion and break up into sects thou hast no part in them in the least: their affair is with Allah: He will in the end tell them the truth of all that they did."

> Quran 23:53: "But people have cut off their affair (of unity) between them into sects: each party rejoices in that which is with itself."

Critical study of Quran

A critical study of Quran must be undertaken. Some of the questions to address were discussed in sections 5 and 6. In addition, the following aspects must also be examined.

- What guidance is offered to the individual, and the manner in which it is to serve the interests of the Ummah?

- What guidance is offered to the Ummah, and what mechanisms are offered to implement that guidance?

- What assumptions are implicitly made regarding the space-time related effects in the human activities?

□ How flexible is the guidance of Quran for the individual as well as the Ummah, in view of the implicit assumptions regarding the space-time factor?

□ What the goal of the guidance is, and how important the ritualistic details of its physical form are?

Definition of the Sunnah

The ambiguities in the definition of the Sunnah and its sources needs to be resolved. Some of the questions to address were discussed in sections 5 and 6. In addition, the following aspects must also be examined.

□ What guidance is offered to the individual, and the manner how is it to serve the interests of the Ummah?

□ What guidance is offered to the Ummah, and what mechanisms are offered to implement that guidance?

□ What assumptions are implicitly made regarding the space-time related effects in the human activities?

□ How flexible is the guidance of Quran for the individual as well as the Ummah, in view of the implicit assumptions regarding the space-time impact?

□ What the goal of the guidance is, and how important the ritualistic details of its physical form are?

We have used a common set of high-level questions to be addressed in the context of Quran and in the context of the Sunnah. Notwithstanding the common phrasing of these questions, their meaning, scope, and impact are widely different in the two cases.

167

8.4 Research in Organization

The program described in this book necessarily requires the development of organized forums to accomplish the various modules of the framework for the mental Hijrah. This aspect has been emphasized throughout the book, and in this chapter, we will reiterate some of those points.

Muslims are rather weak in their ability to get organized under the Islamic principles like the Shura. A tremendous amount of research is therefore needed in this area. Fortunately, the fundamentals of the organizational principals in Islam have been well researched by the Muslim scholars of the 20th century, such as Abul Ala Maududi, Mohammad Iqbal, Ruhullah Khomeni and others. That work is invaluable in giving this effort a starting momentum. The dawn for Muslims of tomorrow is on the horizon. Together, we can paint it beautiful like our glorious past; divided, we can ruin it for our posterity. It will depend on how well we organize.

Fortunately, there exist good examples of organization in the context of today's space-time. No such examples are ever perfect, but they serve as valuable jumpstarts.

Let us consider the democratic approach to organization. It is by no means perfect; however, it has provided a good starting point for many nations. As they gained experience, they adapted the process for the particular space-time conditions of the nation. Thus, the organizational model in the USA, UK, Germany, Japan, and India are commonly referred to as the democratic models. However, they differ in details depending upon the geopolitical realities and the preferences of the local populace.

Within the Islamic context, there exists valuable experience that can be similarly used for a jumpstart. This experience can come from the organizational models used by nation states within the Ummah, for example Turkey, Malaysia, and Iran. These models started with an objective to serve the Ummah, but they took different paths in terms of the detailed resolution of the issues that these countries had to address. Once in place, these models have evolved with the space-time conditions of the nation and the world.

The success of these examples should not be measured in a naïve materialistic manner. Any of the examples stated above, are preferable starting points compared to the non-representative regimes that are rampant within the Ummah today, such as hereditary, military, and oligarchic. The non-representative nature of these regimes exposes the vital interests of the Ummah via the manipulations by the non-Muslim nations. It is indeed a part of the Islamic Jihad for the Muslim masses of such nation states to work in the cause of the Ummah and replace the non-representative regimes. The new regimes must consist of the "people of authority" that come to the "position of authority" through the Islamic process of Shura. Further, it must be possible to replace or remove them from that position by the same process of Shura.

8.4.1 Priority research topics

The organization is impacted at various levels, namely the individual, the society, the nation state, the Muslim Ummah, and the World at large. Below we will briefly discuss each level.

The individual

At the level of the individual, we need to re-orient ourselves along the mental Hijrah defined in this book. In particular, that implies a non-sectarian outlook, and an awareness of the need to uplift the Ummah via active participation in the affairs of the society and the nation state.

The individuals work to establish institutions within the society. Such institutions outlive those individuals who established them, and continue to provide a support system for others, who make their own contributions to the society. The institutions therefore cumulatively grow to transcend the individuals. Such institutions can include the scholarly societies and think tanks. They can promote the kind of research needed for the goals of the nation and the Ummah, serve as watchdogs over the local and national affairs, and devise other action-oriented forums for more effective ways of giving and sharing.

This is part of the Jihad at large.

The society

The organizations in the society provide enabling forums for the individuals to contribute towards the goal of the Ummah.

The individuals in the society need to make deliberate and focused efforts so that the society can organize itself.

This is how the individuals and the society are intertwined.

The nation

At the national level there is a strong need for reorganization. Every nation state must provide strong institutions to ensure that the government indeed is representative of its people. It must also be true to the role of the nation state towards the goals of the Muslim Ummah. These institutions must be in full compliance of Quranic process of Shura.

The process of Shura itself is a topic of research. However, a working model for it must always exist no matter how skeletal it may be. It can improve as the experience-base grows, but the absence of a working implementation of a strong Shura leads to despotic regimes that are apt to compromise the goals of the nation and of the Muslim Ummah.

Such a skeletal model for the process of Shura must include the following high-level Quranic requirements.

o The "people of authority" must come to the "position of authority" through the process of Shura. There is no other acceptable way, so that all hereditary, military, and oligarchic systems of government are manifestly unacceptable.

o It must be possible for the process of Shura to remove the existing "people of authority" and bring in new ones. The only "people of authority" who are not subject to Shura are the Prophets of Allah. However, Mohammad (S) was the last Prophet of Allah. All the "people of authority" today are subject to the process of Shura. That is, they must be placed in the position of authority through the process of Shura and it must

171

be possible to replace or remove them from that position using the same process.

It must be realized that the people who are placed in the position of authority via a process of Shura can also be removed from that position by the same process.

There are very clear Quranic requirements regarding the role and obligations of the "people of authority" in a nation state towards the goals of the Muslim Ummah. Some of these were discussed in chapter 6.

The Ummah

The Ummah today is the collection of the nation states. There is no clear model for the organization of the nation states into the Muslim Ummah. However, some experience-base exists in the form of the organization of the Islamic conference and other similar forums. Such forums are not very functional or effective, because of the utter lack of the process of Shura at the level of the nation states. At the present time, such forums pay little heed to the goals of the Ummah and are largely amenable to manipulation by the non-Muslim forces.

The circumstance is not very encouraging, though it is not entirely unexpected. It is because the experience of the Muslim nations with colonial and neo-colonial monsters has caused disorientation, lack of focus, diminished sense of self-worth, and even doubts about Islam. The damage to the cause of the Ummah is however minimal, which is a living testimony to the strength and greatness of Muslims. The Ummah has remained at the top of the World for over a thousand years. The period of colonization and the continuing period of the neo-colonization are together a small interlude like a nightmare. Muslims are now ready to wake up and shake off this nightmare, notwithstanding the real draconian characters that constitute it.

We shall begin to enact this mental Hijrah, and Allah is our guide.

The world

Even when Muslims are well organized as an Islamic community, they will necessarily share this Earth with those who are not Muslims. The positioning of the Ummah with respect to the rest of the world is of utmost importance. This positioning is not necessarily confrontational. However, the Ummah must be capable and ready to deter and counter any and all threats to its interests.

Since the interests of the Ummah are pivotal for its relationship with the rest of the world, it is of paramount significance to research, understand, and document these interests. Only after these interests have been elaborated in terms of today's space-time, we can meaningfully organize within the global community. Only then we can negotiate with vision, and as is always the case, the Ummah must have the decisive capability to negotiate from the position of strength.

8.4.2 Other research topics

The masses of the nation states within the Ummah must organize forums for the genuine establishment of Shura in order to carry out the obligation to promote the interests of the Ummah. This process of Shura must have at least two ingredients. First, the people in the position of authority must reach there as a result of the process of Shura. This will let Muslims enjoy the fruits of the wisdom behind

173

Quranic guidance. In particular, it will disallow non-representative regimes that are either hereditary or enforced by the military means. Second, the process of Shura must be capable of removing the people from their position of authority so that they continue to behave responsibly towards the interests of the nation and the Ummah. This will stop the mechanisms that the non-representative rulers make available for the non-Muslim nations to systematically compromise the interests of the Ummah in fundamental ways.

The Muslim masses must urgently demand appropriate changes in the ruling structure of their respective nation states. Once the regimes of the nation states within the Ummah begin to represent the Islamic aspirations of their people and the global interests of the Ummah, the glory of Quran will manifest itself. For this task, the masses must strive diligently and patiently and persist in hoping for Allah's help, which surely comes despite the odds, as in Quran 7:128: "Said Moses to his people: "Pray for help from Allah and (wait) in patience and constancy: for the earth is Allah's to give as a heritage to such of his servants as He pleaseth; and the end is (best) for the righteous".

9 Finale

We present a sneak preview of Muslims tomorrow. It is my best effort at analytic continuation into the future.

Allah has set the laws in motion. Whatever happens, or does not happen, does so according to these laws. These laws are an expression of the beauty and the strength that Islam is. The result of the analytic continuation that I offer, as the shape of things to come for the Ummah, is really an expression of my understanding of these laws. This understanding includes the nucleus of the worships in the three dimensions, the overarching Hikmah of Quran, the reality about Muslims, and the reality of the prevailing world order.

There are things I wanted to talk about in this chapter, to add some transparency to my vision of the tomorrow. However, I decided to forgo the opportunity for now. So, the only thing I can offer as the reason for this vision is my unflinching love of Allah and my unblinking trust in the strength of Muslims.

Throughout this book we have discussed a program for the renewal of the Muslim World-View. The discussion has been attempted in an end-to-end manner. Following is a summary of the basic ideas derived and discussed in the course of this work.

9.1 Primary guidance of Allah

The foremost point to realize is that no type of guidance, not even the one from Quran, can be fruitfully used if we do not understand it. The written guidance has to be understood in the context of a particular space-time. Only then it can be made actionable via a sequence of planned steps that form a plan and a process.

It is therefore vital that Allah created us with important capabilities and knowledge. He also breathed His spirit in us. These constitute the human capabilities that form the primary source of guidance. These human faculties must be used in a fundamental way so that any other sources of guidance can be properly understood and then executed.

9.2 Secondary guidance of Allah

The secondary source of guidance is Quran that reached us via the Prophet (S). Quran must therefore be understood using the primary source of guidance, and then the guidance embodied in Quran must be executed within the context of our space-time.

9.3 Tertiary guidance of Allah

The Sunnah is a tertiary source of guidance. It reached us via the oral narration from one person to another, until it was written down. This guidance is harder to understand and should be used only when it carries a clear and unambiguous message within a particular matter in Quran, and in present space-time context. The Sunnah is subjected to the test of its compatibility with Quran. The sources of Sunnah have a much weaker authenticity compared to the authenticity of Quran, and any guidance derived from them should be therefore scrutinized very carefully. In particular, any guidance from the Sunnah that does not sit well with Quran must be either discarded or left alone.

9.4 Worships of Allah

The guidance obtained from any source is eventually translated into actions. The actions are meaningful only in the context of Taqwa, as discussed in Theorem 1 on page 129. Only when performed with Taqwa, these actions are the worships of Allah.

Muslims must adhere to the worships of Allah in all three dimensions, namely physical, ethical, and spiritual. The architectural structure, with these worships as its modules, is intended to promote the interests of the Ummah in relation to the non-Muslim nations, as well as for the spiritual emancipation of the worshipper. Each of these worships is intended with specific objectives that derive from it. If a particular type of worship is neglected, the corresponding objectives are not achieved, as was discussed in Theorem 3 on page 145. The architectural structure is then placed in an unbalanced state, off its equilibrium. The result is that the spiritual emancipation of the worshipper is defective and the position of the Ummah is compromised.

To illustrate this point, we remark that the five pillars of Islam together constitute the worship of Allah in the spiritual dimension, along with the worships that Quran prescribes at the level of the Ummah. The observance of the five pillars alone does not produce a balanced state for the architectural structure that these pillars are intended to support. The worships in the ethical dimension as well as those in the physical dimension are absolutely needed to secure a balanced state for this architecture. The internal dynamics and the feedback mechanisms, between the worships in these three dimensions, are visualized by the law of shadows discussed in Theorem 2 on page 139.

All the above is fruitless without proper organization and forums within the Ummah. The lack of these is currently the weakest link to the achievements of the objectives: of the Ummah as well as the individual worshipper.

9.5 Muslim world-view

There is a very important aspect of Islam that needs to be clearly noted. This is the concept of "Tauheed". It plays a very pivotal role in the Muslim world-view. In particular, this philosophy means the indivisibility of human life.

It is true that there are aspects of human life that can be formalized and contemplated by specialists. Such facets include many dimensions; in particular they include the dimensions of spirituality, psychology, sociology, culture, morality, politics, warfare, and the unity of the humanity. The essential difference between the Euro-American philosophy and the Muslim philosophy lies in the way in which these dimensions combine into the life of the human beings. The Muslim world-view acknowledges the existence of n-dimensions, where n can be finite or infinite depending upon the sophistication of the human endeavor to understand it.

What the Muslim world-view does not accept is a violation of their concept of Tauheed. In particular, they do not accept the postulate that human life can be divided into n aspects and these can be kept separate from one another.

To illustrate this point, let us separate the human life into an aspect called religion and another aspect called state: and let us further postulate that these two aspects can be kept separate from one another. An organization of the human life around this strict separation is very familiar to the Euro American world-view: in fact, the Euro American world-view regards this separation as its admirable characteristic. To the Muslim world-view such an organization strains the human life and subjects it to severe deformations. Such deformations can appear to be small in size, and a simple-minded approach can choose to neglect them. On the other hand, their collective dynamics over extended time periods are so powerful that they disintegrate the human life if it is forced into these unnatural constraints.

A familiar parallel can be drawn with the Newtonian mechanics and the Quantum theory. The Euro-American world-view can be likened to the simplistic description of Nature using the concepts of Newtonian mechanics. In this description, parts of a system can exist independently of the system: and the properties of the system can be accurately understood in terms of its parts. The Quantum theoretic description of a system would state that the constitution of each component involves contributions from all other components. It is therefore impossible to discuss a component in isolation, far less to be able to compose a system from a set of isolated components. This indivisibility of human life is the result of the sophistication with which Muslims view the phenomenon of life, in the light of Quranic concepts.

9.6 Muslim Renaissance

The Euro American world-view is mechanical and devoid of any spirituality in the life of the society (state). This gross over simplification has given rise to countless problems for innocent people. The Muslim world-view takes a wholesome approach and, in particular, recognizes the spiritual dimension to human life. It offers a simple and effective cure to the countless problems that the innocent people are facing in the World today, especially in Europe and Americas.

Our discussion demonstrates that Muslims do not recognize a separation of the society into religion and state: or into any other separation that violates the fundamental principle of the indivisibility of life. A Muslim system therefore freely borrows across the boundaries of the secular and spiritual sides: a boundary that is unnatural and innovated by the simplistic approach taken by the Euro American world-view.

Quran recognizes this wholesome approach. Thus, in the same book we find the worships in the physical, ethical, and spiritual dimensions. Muslims refer to this wholesome and uncorrupted view of life as the "deen", as in Quran 48:28: "It is He who has sent His Apostle with Guidance and the Religion of Truth to proclaim it over all religion: and enough is Allah for a Witness".

This difference in the two world-views is fundamental at a deeper level of human understanding. However, the difference by no means should imply a negation of their interoperability in a certain sense. Thus, Muslims should not shun the benefits that the Euro American world-view has offered. Similarly, the Euro American people should recognize that the approach based on their world-view has paid as much dividends as it had to offer to the society and the individual. It has now entered a region of negative returns, so that it is causing untold sufferings to innocent people. Further advancement is possible by incorporating the Muslim world-view that borrows without taboos, across the artificial barriers between the "religion" and the state.

However, the burden of demonstration is on Muslims: they must take the advantages that the Euro American world-view offers and lead those advantages to the next logical stage in promoting prosperity, peace, and love. They must demonstrate this superiority of their world-view in their own countries; and extend a loving and willing helping hand to the Euro American communities.

Muslims are a most sophisticated and intellectual people, in harmony with the nature. Yet they are simple and modest to the core. Each one of them carries a bag that (s)he regards as a most precious possession. This bag is filled with invaluable gems that are very rare in today's world. They include the human values, the glow of spirituality, and an ever-present consciousness of God (Taqwa).

These human values are intrinsic to humans. They include love, respect, and an urge to give for the benefit of others. They must not be confused with the human rights which is not intrinsic to humans but merely a political instrument. The spirituality gives Muslims a generous and sharing heart in good times and an amazing grace in the face of extreme odds. Taqwa makes the Muslims virtuous in an absolute sense of the word. It also makes them exceptional people without parallel in the Modern world. They are the hope of the World today.

Such beautiful people deserve to be the Khalifah on Earth. That is what they have been almost throughout their history. I said "almost" because over the past century or so they have been dethroned. However, this is a brief period indeed, compared to their history. Unfortunately, it has proved tragic for the World. Ever since Muslims have lost sway, the World has seen two big wars while the threat of the third is ever looming. The spirituality has taken a long break. Lies, deceit, corruption, exploitation and oppression are rampant: Quran refers to these as the Fitnah and the Fasad, as in Quran 8:73.

Mother Earth has been violated while greed and foolishness reined in Europe and Americas.

At this epoch in the human history, Muslims come in for a vital role: to save the humanity from its own greed and foolishness. Hello world: Muslims are now waking up from their slumber.

Muslims are destined to correct the wrongs that the greed and foolishness have brought upon humanity. The spiritual bankruptcy of this self-destructive world-order is breeding more and more greed and foolishness. This ought to stop. Quran has made it a prime mission of Muslims to accomplish this task, as in Quran 3:110.

Muslims have done it in the past, and they shall soon do it again, as Allah wills it so. It will not happen through miracles or Angels. It will happen through the power of knowledge and profound understanding as well as the dedicated efforts (Jihad at large) by the world-wide Muslims.

This century, the first in the new millennium, will see Muslims take control and purify the world-order. The new-world order will take the God given wealth that the mother Earth offers, and will place it in the service of humanity, in a World that will be free from exploitation and oppression. These are the fundamental practices of Islam: to seek wealth with a God conscious mindset (Salat) and to share it in the love of humanity (Zakat). Accomplishing this will be Jihad at large, and it will require a great deal of Ijtehad.